T0131598

Soul's Homecoming

An Empath's Journey to Inner Wisdom

KATHARINE DONOVAN KANE

BALBOA.PRESS

A DIVISION OF HAY HOUSE

Balboa Press books may be ordered through booksellers or by contacting:

Balboa Press
A Division of Hay House
1663 Liberty Drive
Bloomington, IN 47403
www.balboapress.com
844-682-1282

Print information available on the last page.

ISBN: 978-1-9822-7727-7 (sc)
ISBN: 978-1-9822-7726-0 (hc)
ISBN: 978-1-9822-7725-3 (e)

Library of Congress Control Number: 2021923117

Balboa Press rev. date: 12/02/2021

Katharine Donovan Kane has the remarkable gift of painting pictures with words that completely captivates and transforms the reader. In her book, *Soul's Homecoming,* she creates a path of inner exploration and transformation that connects everyday life to our intuitive selves in a way that is inspiring and magical. I found myself repeatedly saying "Yes!" out loud as she exquisitely describes the journey to know ourselves, others, and the spirit-filled world we live in. I highly recommend this book as a magnificent tool for personal transformation.

Kathryn Severns Avery
Coach, Speaker, and Author of *Your Countdown to Retirement, Tiara Training,* and *The 15 Minute Fairy Godmother*

In a world of movement and constant change, there is a call for stillness that so many are ready to hear. This beautiful work breathes life into this truth. With deep reflections from her life, artistic pieces from her journeying, and advice about how to embrace these healing tools, Kane brings us a powerful narrative to support us in exploring our own dive into our inner wisdom.

Cythera Wilkerson, L.Ac.
Owner, *Medicine of the Heart*

This book is packed with poetic and deeply personal invitations by Katharine Donovan Kane into the "thin places" of our own heart. By sharing her own experiences as an empath on a journey to spiritual wholeness, Kane moves us from the thinking mind into a world of symbol, magic, and synchronicity. This book will serve as a wonderful companion for anyone working with highly sensitive clients, or who is discovering this magnificent "way of knowing" in themselves.

Louisa W. Foster, PsyD, RDT/BCT
Founder and Director of *The Center for Mindful Living*
Co-Founder, *The Midwest Drama Therapy Institute*

Dedication

With gratitude to Conor Kane Lane, who read my initial manuscript pages and whose intuitive spirit gave me the enthusiastic encouragement that inspired the rest.

Contents

Acknowledgments

With much appreciation to Kathryn Severns Avery, Casey Gammon, Nancy Huslage, Andrea Michels, and Cythera Wilkerson for your critiques and support. Special thanks to Ron Goodman, who generously understood my hours at the kitchen table writing and watching the backyard birds.

And with love to my children—Madelaine, Erin, Colleen, and Conor. I asked to be blessed with a sign and was gifted with all of you.

Foreword

This is the beautiful narrative of Katharine's own soul's homecoming; a powerful, compelling poetics of one spiritual journey that promises to be transformative for everyone who wants to live life to the full.

The author, an experienced spiritual life coach and dream facilitator, weaves for you, the reader, a treasure-tapestry of insights with multi-coloured threads from Jungian psychology, synchronicities, Irish inheritance, monastic zen and Christian practices, the vibrations of nature and the earth, rituals and active imagination particularly through dream-catching.

Céad mile fáilte to a practical, informative meditation that will awaken the spirit of the mystic in every seeker and searcher, expertly guided by the erudite imaginative writing of Katharine Donovan Kane who has truly travelled this soul journey herself.

As an Irish Inter-faith spiritual director myself, I warmly welcome this contemporary Book of Wisdom. I *highly* recommend it to every person who, not only feels called to a deeper inner understanding of being but, who is also open and willing to embrace this new beginning right away.

St. Augustine's conversion was sparked by a voice which commanded him to *'tolle, lege'* – take and read. Likewise, to every person in pursuit of truth and beauty, I invite you to open up and carefully read this book and I promise that you will be truly transformed.

Take and read now and postpone **your** soul's homecoming no longer!

Rev. Nóirín Ní Riain PhD
Glenstal Abbey, Murroe, Co. Limerick
Samhain 29th 2021

Introduction

Beaconed by an inner clock to awaken, my eyes slowly open and search the darkened room as my body remains heavy with sleep, reluctant to follow. Dawn's misty light slips through the East-facing window and rests gently on the wall, like the shimmering gray tones of the bedroom mirror. This is the moment of day when the barrier between the worlds of what our eyes can see and what our imaginations can sense is both subtle and lucid. Dawn is an important time, and the creative energy it offers is not to be missed. It is said we receive our best inspirations when the birds haven't quite awakened. There's a hush in the woods outside, though sometimes you might hear a barred owl's deep hoot. Or perhaps crows begin to call for each other. You may be one of those people who likes the late night, when skylight darkens and the red fox calls. No matter, it is a time to reflect on a question like the one American poet Mary Oliver asks in her poem "The Summer Day." "Tell me," she writes, "what is it you plan to do with your one wild and precious life?"

Whatever your preference, the spiritual and poetic journeys we are on as we search the nooks and crannies of our minds and the whimsical whisperings of our spirits will help us find our ways. Using your own inner map as a guide to your soul's homecoming, you will become more and more attuned to your unique signals. We all travel through darkness and lonely times in the pursuit of personal awareness. And at times we lament that the goddesses and gods have abandoned us in this uncomfortable, unfamiliar space. But this discomfort can be an opening or represent a threshold—in other words, a liminal space. Liminal, derived from the Latin word *limen*, meaning a border or doorway between one thing and another, is a reminder that in the breath between words is a place full of meaning. It is time to pause and hear the messages given to us in these spaces.

Take a moment to close your eyes and inhale deeply. Let your breath out slowly. Inhale again. Hold the in breath for a few seconds, and then slowly release, pausing at the end of the exhalation as if waiting for all the air to gather itself. Do this several more times, and then look and listen again. We receive messages all the time as we actively transition between what was and what's coming next. Like the legend of a map, our intuitions, night dreams and daydreams, ancestral memories, and the collective unconscious—a term coined by psychiatrist and psychoanalyst Carl G. Jung representing the deep-rooted shared essence of human nature—are guideposts along our paths. Once you decide to embark on the journey, you will notice a desire bubbling up at this vital threshold as if your life depended on it.

To understand the keys of this inner map, it helps to learn the language of these distinct messages. Dreams and visions communicate with us in signs, symbols, and metaphors. There are synchronicities to watch out for as well as intuitions and thoughts that come to mind when you least expect them. And what about the body? The vibrations, the heartaches, the goose bumps, the butterflies in your stomach, and the sudden concern that grips your heart space are all messages.

Coaches, dream workers, therapists, physicians, and energy healers such as certified Reiki practitioners are some of the trained specialists available to companion us through this intricate labyrinth. The question becomes, how do we build an intimate relationship with our own signals emerging from the palatial landscape within? We find ourselves at the base of the mountain, looking up and wondering about this journey we're contemplating. It seems daunting. Shaking our heads we doubtfully back away thinking, *Maybe I should have coffee first and think this over.* Yet there is that inner whisper as subtle as the early morning light. It is nudging us to awaken.

This book is the story of my soul's homecoming. By sharing my experiences, I hope to inspire you to take up your own unique map and find the way to your soul's home. Maps, for me, are a bit of a conundrum. I love them. I enjoy the idea of picking a destination, choosing the route, and anticipating points of interest along the way. And yet for my figurative life's map, I've learned that frequently I needed to live life before I could see where to go. A lot has happened to me: deaths of loved ones, birthing children, university degrees, divorce, job loss, and numerous other new beginnings. I have seen many of the detours as well as guideposts along the road.

We all have a wild tale to tell, and as a deep listener, I am passionate about windswept stories. I am a guide of inner exploration who has trained for and obtained the required navigational skills. These proficiencies as a coach, dream facilitator, and spiritual companion are important, to be sure, but what I really bring is myself as an empath. I am highly sensitive to gut feelings as well as the energy frequencies of people, animals, and my surroundings. As an intuitive with insight into dreams and meaningful signs, I have learned to notice the kind of signals that pop into awareness like the unexpected flicker of tiny fireflies on a summer's night. I embrace the larger intuitive hits when they come, like when inexplicable uneasiness gripped me weeks before I lost my job. I became alert and aware of the energy around me, conscious that a dynamic shift was taking place. When the job transition occurred, while still difficult, it was met with less heartache and an understanding that a new opportunity was presenting itself. I learned that to be open and to listen and receive cues while practicing awareness are key elements of going on an inner journey. They are essential to being mindful that you are on the road in the first place.

Reading signs in nature brings a special wisdom. Imagine if a hawk appeared in your backyard one day or in the tree outside your apartment window. And being the territorial creatures that they are, the hawk begins to appear on a regular basis. You are fortunate to have noticed the hawk who quietly observes. Undisturbed, it patiently waits on its perch until the right moment arrives for change. To hear the hawk's cry is magical. It's calling out to you to pay attention. What about the crows that, after noticing this same hawk, begin to loudly protest, cawing and swooping down toward the large, calm bird to scare it away? Crows often fly in flocks, sometimes called a murder of crows, calling to each other as they fan out in the sky on their searches and rescue missions. They are birds of protection. Ever wonder if they are trying to get you to stop and notice what they can see? How often do we hear them and tuck their calls into the background noise of our daily activities? What if on a nature walk one day, out of nowhere a deer with antlers poking the air like giant antennae came charging toward you on the same path you were following? This happened to me one morning as I marched down the wooded path upset at a challenging conversation I had just experienced. Startled, I came to a quick stop and watched the buck gallop toward me. Frozen in place, I saw it leap away and disappear into the woods. I looked to where it had gone, but there was no deer, only the silence of trees and bushes. In nature one animal calls for our attention, another silently awaits our notice, and another shocks us out of our reveries. They selflessly serve as protectors, mystery holders, and majestic reminders leading us back to the primal understanding of ourselves.

And there's that moment during the day when you stop and pause to think of someone special. Your finger hovers above your phone, ready to send them a message, only to simultaneously receive a "How are you?" text from that person. These synchronistic occurrences are easily dismissed, but they are powerful reminders that a sense of mystery surrounds us.

It's all about learning to pay attention to the unique language of what philosopher, theologian, and Sufism expert Henry Corbin calls "Mundus Imaginalis," an imaginal realm, a world accessed through our imaginations, where synchronicities, creativity, and visions exist. The Celts have a similar understanding of this realm called the Otherworld, a place beyond the veil yet contiguous with our physical reality, that communicates with us through dreams, symbols, music, and archetypal images.

Suppose we began to look at life as a fascinating emergence of signs, symbols, and inspired imagination. Empaths and highly sensitive persons are especially good at paying attention to these kinds of signals. We all are experiencing an important point in history when we empaths are needed to openly share our intuitive gifts of introspection, feeling, and perceiving. Our world as we know it bestows special recognition to the majority inhabitants of doers, overtly expressive, straightforward, and unreserved population. I propose a world where many voices—both the poetic and the literal—have a place. To create a more balanced worldview, empaths are encouraged to learn an awareness of nature's voice, to pay attention to special moments when insight emerges, and to articulate this wisdom with our creative expressions. This gift is no longer a curiosity or something to ignore in ourselves.

As a human species we are only one part of the whole natural realm. The woods are alive with trees, birds, and animals who, like us, have their own vital intelligence. Empaths and highly sensitive persons have an opportunity to observe and reflect on the mystery being revealed, not just for their own sakes, but for the whole of nature.

What is your inner wisdom saying? I welcome you to unleash your awareness and share it with a world that so desperately needs your distinctive inspiration. Let us enter this magical time together and delight in paying special attention to the nuggets of bliss, as well as the gut-wrenching challenges, while our unique insight reveals its mysterious voice.

It's sacred ground. I can hear the crow making a ruckus, beaconing us to notice what it sees and to pay attention. It is our protector, our guide, as we begin the journey.

Chapter 1

Allowing Inner Wisdom to Emerge

I WAS BORN IN OCTOBER IN THE NORTHERN HEMISPHERE. IT IS A special time of year for me, and not just because of my birthday. Autumn's vibrant colors of yellow, burnt orange, and blazing red are as inspiring as the season's cool, crisp air is appealing. Yet that is only part of what draws me in. Fall is a sacred time; it is the season of Samhain *(sah-win)*.

Samhain is celebrated as the beginning of a new year within the Celtic tradition. It is a time when a tangible sense of presence is felt, and imagination becomes an important threshold. It is believed to be a season when the Otherworld, a world just beyond our seeing or immediate understanding, becomes more readily available to us. That is, if we're paying attention. At the heart of Irish mythology, the Otherworld is a traditional belief born out of a lived experience that comes from a deep relationship with the land. The edge separating our everyday perceptions and sensations from the Otherworld is said to be especially thin during Samhain. It is a season when we acknowledge ancestors who have passed and when we can access the wisdom they left for us to discover.

The connection between our heightened ancestral awareness with their messaging to us is ripe at this time. My mother passed in early fall, so it makes sense that she comes to mind then. When I smell an aroma in the air, a scent that is the perfume she wore, I stop to look around, thinking to find her. When I don't see her, sorrow arises, clenching my throat. But ironically, a smile emerges as well. Moments like this are warm hugs from where she is now, a place of combined ancestral energy wrapping itself around me like a soft shawl to comfort the chill.

The season of Samhain offers a bridge between what we know and what is yet to be known. It is an opportunity to cross the threshold and engage with both memories and sacred intelligence.

The Otherworld encompasses a realm as natural and as real as our own. It is a place of sacred intelligence that exists side by side with our perceived actuality. I can always count on my ability to sense the Otherworld making its presence known through signs of wonder, an awareness of knowing, or perhaps a feeling of connectedness as I walk among the trees in the woods. This awareness is available to us all the time, not just when we invoke its presence during prayer or meditation. I remember watching my daughter, Madelaine, participate in a lyric opera accompanied by a small orchestra. She sang the role of Mimi in *La Bohème*. As I listened, my emotion for her was so strong that I was afraid she would sense it. Instead, I concentrated on her outer frame rather than directly at her face. My eyes squinted when a white aura appeared in a subtle flicker of air. I continued to look at her edges as Madelaine performed Lucia, revealing herself as Mimi to Rodolfo. At that moment, my heart knew that her voice was the bridge between her physicality and her other side-by-side reality. She was connected to her inner truth, and I was seeing the shimmering energy surrounding her.

Importantly, as mentioned earlier, the Otherworld is a sacred space that communicates with us through the language of symbols, metaphors, and archetypes. "The voice" coming forth from Madelaine embodied the archetype of alignment, truth, and inner essence—a universal experience potentially understood by the collective. It can be life changing when listening to someone use his or her voice in full relationship with the individual's truth.

**Standing inside an ancient monk's hut on
Inis Mór, looking out toward the light.**

Samhain celebrates inherited memories. This Celtic season occurs at a time of year when many other traditional ancestral remembrances and devotions to spirits take place throughout the world. Various Indigenous People of North America, for instance, commemorate their heritages, the land, and their ancestors during the month of November. *Día de los Muertos*, the Day of the Dead, is a celebration important in Mexico and throughout Latin America. All Saints Day and All Souls Day are Christian holy days widely observed. In late-summer and early fall there are other observances such as the *Gai Jatra* in Nepal, the *Bhoot Chaturdashi* in Bengal, and the *Hungry Ghost Festival* in many Asian countries. Then there is the late-summer *Obon* festival in Japan.

I lived in Kyoto when I was introduced to the Obon, the Festival of the Dead. My memory conjures up a younger version of me dressed in a lightweight yukata, a summer kimono. The brilliant white and deep-blue floral design of the yukata was simple yet bold. I felt beautiful in it. I recall the smell of the garment and the feel of it on my skin as delicate as washi paper lanterns. And I noticed how my senses picked up details I normally ignored. Dressed in the yukata, a gift from my students, allowed me to feel like I truly belonged with them as we attended the Obon festival together. A magical ambience was created by lanterns that adorned the pagoda at Daigo-ji Temple like elegant tinsel. Dressed in decorative attire, participants took part in Bon Odori dances in an elaborate acknowledgment of ancestral presence. At dusk, hundreds of paper lanterns with candles were set afloat on the water below the Togetsu-kyo, the moon crossing bridge, to send the lamented family members back to the other side.

I first moved to Japan during Obon festival time as an English teacher. I didn't speak Japanese when I first arrived in Kyoto, so I needed to rely on my intuitive senses to help me understand, communicate, and deeply appreciate what was happening. While standing on the Togetsu-kyo bridge with my new students, I had an unexpected association with my experience living in Ireland years earlier. As I watched the paper lanterns and thought of the ancestors being honored, there was a real sense of presence, of otherworldliness. It occurred to me I had felt the same in Ireland when I learned the deep connection the Irish have to the land, which holds their ancestral inheritance. I felt a chill on that hot, late-summer evening as I stared at the flickering lanterns float away down the river. I realized that two ancient peoples shared the same essential sacred intelligence.

The question then becomes, how do we ignite a connection to the ancestral wisdom in our families of origin or perhaps with the spirit of the land where we find ourselves living? Ancestral energies and sacred intelligence live in and around us. One's intuition becomes the entrée to their messages. Intuition is expanded by actively using our imaginations in creative pursuits such as writing poetry, engaging in music, photography, or simply working in the garden. This doesn't require that we produce professional-quality outcomes. Rather, it is by delving into the creative process that the thinking-mind falls away, and the heart-mind connects with a unique wealth of insight that heightens our intuitive senses. We can also engage inner wisdom through somatic bodywork; that is, being in tune with what we are sensing and feeling. This is done through various meditative techniques as well as simple breathing exercises. The practice of intentional meditation, along with using your senses and intuition, will help you more easily recognize instances of greater knowing.

When we weave our intellectual, sensuous, and spiritual understandings in purposeful ways, we encounter a time out of time. It is an opportunity to feel the presence of the other, to hear the whisperings, and to practice leaning into a greater knowing. For some, greater knowing is another way of expressing God, the Soul of the universe, or the Source of being. It is in this way that sacred intelligence expresses the shared essence of human nature. However you define the holy or divine for yourself, connecting with this part of the inner landscape helps to tap into a fuller understanding of one's true self, or Self with a capital S.

A Map to Inner Knowing

By using imagination in my meditation practice to call in a deeper knowing of my ancestors, I could imagine that those before me had an intimate relationship to Earth. I often refer to Earth as more than the ground on which we live. She encapsulates many characteristics: land, sea, air, as well as the constellations living in the sky. My ancestors spent a fair amount of time on the rough seas around Ireland's west coast. For certain they were impacted by Earth's storms when they worked the land. What is so interesting to me is that when traveling the waterways, they needed to read the moods of the sea, the mindset of the weather, and be able to understand how changes in the sky affected the stability of their boats. They had a deep sense of where they were, how to negotiate with their surroundings, and to be prepared for changes in the sea's temperament. Reading signs in nature and translating the meaning were key to survival.

While on a ferry ride between Rossaveel and the Isle of Inis Mór, I could call forth visions of my ancestors sailing these same waters. Earlier in the day, a strong storm had threatened our boat ride. The clouds were still dark and rumbling. Heading out of the harbor I stood at the bow and watched Inis Mór loom larger on the horizon as we bounced from wave to wave, slapping our way across Galway Bay. Here is where I made the connection that my strong affinity to maps was due in part to my ancestors. I like the paper ones, the ones you hold in your hands and feel their texture and folds with your fingers. I chuckle as I write this because I recall insistently telling my children that "You need to know how to read maps in case your electronic devices don't work!" Paper maps are nothing like their GPS electronic cousins. I like to open the accordion folds and flatten it out to see the big picture. This way I have a sense of where the road is leading and what we will encounter along the way. If detours are needed—and they often are—I already can see what roads are good alternatives. And yes, I have learned to read the metaphorical sea disposition. If I'm your navigator, there is little to worry about. I will find the way.

As I set out on a journey to find my own inner wisdom, sometimes disguised as patterns of being or challenges arising in my current life, I realize I have to access another type of map. This isn't something already plotted by cartographers and laid out in grids with street names and compass directional signs. Instead, I'll need to pave a new road. Unlike the tools used by the ancient Greeks, when today's mapmakers create new maps, they look at satellite images, understand the demographic information of people who live in the area, and pay attention to things like bodies of water and the effects of weather on the environment. Surveyors are sent in to take measurements and understand the boundaries of the land. After all the data is collected, creatives step in and sketch out preliminary graphs and images of what the map may look like.

Similarly, like these professional mapmakers, sketching out our pathways to wisdom entails spending some time getting to know our inner landscapes. It may involve a look at life's big picture to understand our personal stories and how we choose to show up in the world. We take note of successes, times and places of learning, as well as how we weather the inner storms and the choppy water of what life offers to us. Once we set out to map a deeper understanding of who we are, we may discover a connection to our ancestors that leads us into our deeper sources of knowing. From here we begin to create stories worthy of our next chapters, honoring the hard-worn paths our ancestors trod so we may move forward intellectually and spiritually toward our true norths, our centers.

Discovery: I'm an Empath

One of my greatest joys is having studied with Jungian analysts and theologians at the Haden Institute in North Carolina. Haden holds its workshops and seminars at Kanuga Conference Center, near Asheville, nestled in the appropriately named Blue Ridge Mountains. This mass of undulating rock was pushed up out of the earth, and for hundreds of millions of years, has stood abidingly. Grandfather Mountain, considered one of the oldest in the world, rests among these formations. The Blue Ridge Mountains are named because of its naturally occurring isoprene, a hydrocarbon that is released by the pines, hemlocks, oaks, maples, spruce, and other wondrous trees. When seen from a distance shrouded in hazy mountain mist, these ancient Earth-ancestors draw our attention with their regal blue. Kanuga resides there. On my first visit I was told that Kanuga is a thin place. "Thin place." I had heard this expression from my Irish and Scottish friends and was curious about the term. "Thin" refers to a physical place on Earth where the veil between the worlds is believed to be delicate and more accessible. You could say a mystical place. What better setting to be in to learn about the Jungian aspects of the human inner map than this place that is reminiscent of Samhain, the bridge between the known and yet to be known.

It was here that I finally accepted my gifts as an empath. I said it out loud. I heard myself declare it and clear enough for others to witness. It came as goose bumps, sensing presence as I walked in the woods, or rubbing my stomach as I became aware that the mountains had a story to tell. I found myself inquiring about the history of Kanuga and the geography surrounding it. I wondered about the Civil War activity there more than one hundred fifty years ago. Or perhaps it's the enduring spirit of this Western mountain region of North Carolina that still holds the tears and perseverance of the Eastern Band of the Cherokee Nation. I finally stopped running from myself and faced the reality that I felt in my body that the earth, the land of these Blue Ridge Mountains, was holding a memory, and I could sense it.

As an empath, I have known the feeling of perceiving more than what appears on the surface of things, of having heightened fatigue when around large assemblies, or sometimes absorbing the emotional output of people around me. Both scientific and spiritual texts have documented this particular hypersensitivity, which can manifest by an amplified tuning in to energy fields or electrical currents that encircle all sentient beings and the earth. Not all empaths have the same talents at reading these energies, yet it is clear that our tendencies to be overwhelmed by crowds or by sensing the feelings of others, coupled with the fear of being misunderstood or criticized for these abilities, encourage us to hide our gifts.

Being viewed as overly sensitive to life in general or not trusting your own innate gifts teaches you to keep quiet about your feelings. This can be especially true if these occurrences begin in childhood, when it is hard to explain what is happening and causes you to second-guess your experiences. The family's openness to discussing a child's view of what may seem impossible can determine how long it takes to live openly as an empath. I recall one of my first glimpses at unusual experiences—and keeping it hidden. I was eight years old. I didn't understand what was happening. Nor did I have the language to describe it. As a child, I never shared the encounter that took place in the wake of my father's death. I was deeply sad and alone in my room. It was a nightly ritual. I wondered aloud why he needed to go and asked him to come home. Sometime after falling asleep, I suddenly awoke to sense a strong energy rushing toward me. I knew it was my father, and half asleep I sat in my bed frozen and alarmed, looking at the window across the room, the portal that brought him to me. I stared at the window and held my breath as his energy slowed and dissipated. I reminisced later in life that this energy somehow knew I wasn't ready to understand, and so it left. It became an important memory but was locked away for a long time. *Who would believe it?* I remembered thinking. Mostly, though, I was a young child who quietly observed. I hadn't heard many stories from family members about their experiences of my father's passing. We didn't speak of it. In my young mind the experience became an ending rather than an opening into other possibilities.

I am an ambivert, sometimes called an outgoing introvert. This is to say I love people; I like being with them and getting to know them by listening to their stories. I can be around large crowds or attend parties for a short time without too much disturbance to my well-being. However, like all empaths, I require quiet—a lot of it. Too much loud interaction or loud music depletes my energy. I get exhausted sooner than non-empaths. I occasionally need to escape to the sandy ocean shore, walk a solitary path in a wooded area, or spend hours with hands in the dirt tending my garden in order to replenish inner resources.

My strongest empathic gifts show up as an intuitive, using my senses to read gut feelings, and as a dream empath by remembering many of my dreams and untangling them for deeper understanding. I have a strong connection to birds, and as an earth empath, I seek and feel the vibrations of the land and its messages. Being at Kanuga, the thin place I now know in North Carolina's Blue Ridge Mountains, sharing with my colleagues at the Haden Institute has offered me an extended family of other highly sensitive folks who see and experience life in similar ways.

There are empaths who are like sponges, absorbing the emotional projections of others. And there are those who can read the physical well-being of others or sense the presence of persons who have passed to the other side. We have special gifts as empaths and have good reason to be shy about sharing with others. We have experienced people in our lives who were not accepting of these inherent gifts. Sometimes societal norms or mainstream religious communities do not condone what may appear as unusual occurrences. The possibility of being shunned by individuals, our families, or perhaps our livelihoods is good cause to shut down or even suppress these essential parts of our inner wisdom. But it is time to give voice to our abilities. The world has gotten into a tight spot by predominantly using the logical mind and linear thinking patterns. Persons with gifts of connection to the earth, of accessing dream-time realms, or using high-level intuition to make decisions that serve the global community have been holding back for too long. We have spent most of our lives sick or mentally stressed for trying to fit into the world's preferred mode of operation.

Puzzle Pieces of the Psyche

Jungian analyst Kathleen Wiley, who is often a main presenter at the Haden Institute, has a practice of standing startlingly barefooted at the podium, displaying a bright smile as she explains Jungian theories. She is fond of reminding us that having her feet in physical contact with the earth is essential for her. She is so at ease without shoes in front of the group that it is beguiling. Her audiences are accustomed to it; her lectures make you feel comfortable and relaxed. In the same way, I take every opportunity to go without shoes and to be in physical contact with where I am walking. It is a reminder that wherever my feet are planted, the rocks and trees have stood abidingly for millennia and, in turn, have something to teach me. I encourage you to do this too. Feel the cool sensation of wet grass or the warmth of dry grainy sand. Wherever you are, allow the earth to seep its energy into you. Like my ancestors who learned how to read the sky to keep themselves safe on the water, we need to discover how to connect with the earth in order to establish balance in life.

In addition to an outer connection to our worlds, it is important to have a basic awareness of how the psyche plays a part in the inner landscape. Jung said, "The psychology of every individual would need its own manual." I like the word "manual" since it reminds me of my love of maps. Awareness and acceptance of the whole assortment of our inner characteristics is what Jung refers to as "individuation." It is an ongoing personal unfolding of self-realization whereby we aspire toward a balanced relationship with all the aspects of self and Self. According to Jung, the self is regarded as the ego, or the center of consciousness, while the Self is seen as the unification of consciousness and the unconscious. The Self is also seen as the archetype of wholeness, or as Jung says, the, "totality of a person's being," and is often symbolized as a circle.

Our conscious mind reaches outward to the collective consciousness and inward to the persona, ego, and body consciousness to assemble what is called the psyche. The collective consciousness, what society knows about itself, informs an individual's story. The ego is the nucleus around which our thoughts, feelings, senses, and intuitions circulate. The ego is an essential piece of one's whole puzzle. It helps us to understand our places in the world. Too often, however, we think of ego as the only important aspect of our beings.

There are other personal facets at play. The persona, for example, is the public relations department of the ego. It likes to wear masks to show others what we want them to see about ourselves. The persona is good at adapting to the outside world. And then there is body consciousness, which echoes the sensations and perceptions it picks up from the internal and external worlds. These aspects are all part of our conscious minds, a component of the psyche. What we know about ourselves and what stage of life we are in will influence an awareness of how the ego, the body, the persona, and the unconscious interact with each other.

I am the seventh of ten children from a New York City Irish family. Because my father died when I was eight years old, I grew up in a household with a single mom in a time that didn't have many societal resources to assist her. Right there, in that one sentence, is a jam-packed story of my wounded ego and a persona that learned to shield herself with a protective image that was tough, argumentative, and a mask reflecting someone who could handle whatever life dished out. Our stories are impacted by body sensation awareness and emotional reactivity to our immediate environments as well as to the levels of unconsciousness that are present in our inner worlds but are not yet known.

Remember the mapmaker? She instructs us that it takes more than a one-time satellite flyover to collect basic facts to lay out the grid. In the same way, your personal history is nuanced, requiring more thoughtful examination. We must also pay attention to the metaphorical effects of weather on our landscapes. In other words, we need to distinguish our personal versus inherited stories. How do we interpret the emerging messages from the unconscious parts of ourselves making a ruckus? Jung explains that the personal unconscious represents everything we know about ourselves but have forgotten. These can be complexes, emotions, perceptions, wishes, or patterns below the surface that will eventually reemerge into the conscious mind when we are ready to deal with them.

The collective unconscious fascinates me the most. I am always interested in how major global events or changes in the natural world reflexively impact who I am and how I interact with the worldview. Even more mysterious, and worthy of my curiosity, is how the collective unconscious of my ancestors touches me.

I remember when I was just shy of eighteen and had recently graduated from high school. My mother knew that my high school experience was filled with the upheaval of the late 1960s both in the general society and in my family. She sent me off to Ireland to spend the summer with my aunt and uncle. I had never traveled abroad; the longest journey I remember taking was going from Long Island to New York City to visit my grandmother. For sure I had never been on a plane. It was a surreal experience going to Ireland. I remember pleading with my mother to come with me. It wasn't possible for her to leave her responsibilities in New York, so off I went, a confused and reluctant teenager, with my very first passport in hand.

I sat next to a woman from Texas who, like me, was flying for the first time. She was traveling to Ireland to meet her new grandchild and nervously held my hand for what seemed like the whole way across the ocean. Six hours later, after sharing life stories, we made a bumpy landing at Shannon Airport. We deplaned on to the tarmac since there was no jetway. Atop the plane's staircase I was met with a brisk gust off the River Shannon. I stood mesmerized by hues of green I never knew existed. Breathing in a strong earthy aroma, I heard an unexpected voice in my head. The voice said, *Finally, you have come home.* As a teenager, I had no idea what had happened. What did it mean to come home? Even more perplexing as I had not yet recognized myself as an empath, I kept this whispered message to myself. I certainly had no idea what to think of it. It took me a long time to acknowledge to myself that I heard this message and to understand what it all meant. At the time I remember thinking, *Could it have been my ancestors speaking to me?* If I could have spoken to my younger self, I would have answered yes.

More important, what surfaced was the message of coming home. Was there something I saw that conveyed an association of home? I grew up on Long Island, where you are never too far from water whether the Long Island Sound or the Atlantic Ocean. So I recognized the familiar sea air on my cheeks the moment I deplaned. I breathed in a pungent aroma of Ireland's rich brown earth, and I knew farmlands were nearby. Both islands have in common that their lands are partially glacial deposits of clay. Nevertheless, I knew there was a unique difference in what I was experiencing. It was certainly a new place, yet what I saw and felt instantly triggered something deep in my unconscious. It awakened an inherited memory offered to me by Ireland's special energy as a thin place, where the Otherworld captures the imagination and encourages a new beginning.

At present, with the benefit of a lifetime of experiences, I can say confidently something was calling me then—as it calls to me today—to be conscious of thin places and allow my empathic nature to engage with memories and sacred intelligence.

When we are open to our whole beings and allow the unconscious to emerge, thoughts and feelings come up that we may not recognize or that we haven't seen in a long time. One's shadow side is a good example of what is shown to us. It is the part of our inner landscapes that are often familiar with fear, and the parts of ourselves we dislike the most or like to ignore. When we overlook our shadow sides, they tend to reveal themselves as overreactions to encounters we have, moody feelings, or by us blaming others. In general, opening up to this part of ourselves seems like an unwelcome, frightening, and scary proposition. Ironically, though, our shadow sides are our good friends. They teach us things about ourselves that are challenges, to be sure, yet they help us grow.

Another way to interact with shadow is by accepting the darkness as being helpful, even comforting. When we started life we were in darkness, getting ready, forming, becoming. Then came the light of day. We literally and figuratively emerged from the womb as new creations. Without that time in darkness, we would not be able to actualize fully as infants. Becoming friendly with your shadow self allows a curiosity about it, and instead of being critical, we begin to face our shadows with impartiality.

Overall, we are complex beings. If you believe you are an empath, taking the time to investigate and explore the inner landscape brings a peace to your soul. I believe that if we spend time to fit together the details that encompass these inner puzzle pieces, especially the ones that lurk in the unconscious, then we can minimize unwelcome effects. Each of us has scattered pieces of ourselves due to dramas in our lifetimes or in previous lifetimes. This disintegration of self makes us feel out of balance. There is a gratification in putting those pieces into perspective, so we may embrace ourselves wholly as empaths.

While embarking on an exploration of inner wisdom, it is valuable to know the signposts marking our personal landscapes as well as how the collective unconscious affects our psyches. In order for us to allow our inner selves space to grow, it is helpful to familiarize ourselves with the world of signs, symbols, and metaphors. The key to understanding our own inner landscapes and to broaden our awareness of the Otherworld's messages is to learn its language.

Katharine Donovan Kane

Journey Exercise

Close your eyes. Get physically grounded to the earth by connecting to it with your bare feet. Then breathe deeply three times, holding each inhalation and exhalation for a second or two. This is a good place to begin the practice of deep awareness.

Journey Question

When do you recognize gut feelings in your body? Does this intuitive awareness trigger a memory, an experience long forgotten, or perhaps one inherited by familial patterns? How are you allowing your inner wisdom to emerge?

Chapter 2

Learning the Language

THERE ARE VARIOUS WAYS TO LISTEN, SENSE, AND FEEL THE wisdom of the inner landscape, to know this aspect of ourselves. Daily meditations that focus on deep breathing and nature walks in a wooded area near my home are a few ways I refresh my physical and spiritual reserves. I am fortunate to live near a neighborhood of trees. I call it my neighbor-wood. Pileated woodpeckers, crows, barred owls, blue jays, and ground-loving wood thrushes reside there. Aging tulip trees, red oaks, and downed tree trunks are home to chipmunks and places for deer to hide. As an earth empath, I can't think of a better setting to experience quiet and practice awareness of my surroundings, listening to bird calls, catching glimpses of the elusive urban deer darting out from behind the bushes, and taking in the silence. Its stillness helps me tune into the vibrations of the earth.

There have been times when I found it hard to stay open to my intuition. So many stories of hardship, of sickness, of job loss, of sorrow sometimes overload my senses. I escape to the nearby neighbor-wood to cleanse my mind. My thoughts wander as the crunch of leaves beneath my hiking shoes echoes through the trees. I catch myself thinking I should be seeking employment instead of the walk. Yet in all honesty, I know I am rehashing leftover guilt, perhaps insecurity, from my own recent pandemic-related job loss. I am grateful, though, that my inner observer notices I've ambled into a moment of stressful self-judgment. I think, *Hmmm. Perhaps my mind is not always the best way to discover the new pathway in front of me.* I decide to do an experiment.

If I can't think my way out of a "should have" dilemma, what else am I able to do? I recall that I often use my hands to redirect the energy from my brain activity to my body. In the past I would weave rugs or use crayons, color pencils, and other materials to fashion creative objects. Gardening, getting my hands dirty in the soil was even better. I would look at the land around me and imagine a patch of perennials, bushes with berries, or a miniature Japanese maple. And then I'd get to work bringing this dream to life. After spending hours digging, racking, mowing, and planting, my body was exhausted. I was physically tired, yet I noticed that my whole self was rested.

Drawing on my own experience, it is time to help my body remember that it has a key role to play in helping me enter into intuitive knowing. Body messages are my doorway into inner wisdom, where synchronicities emerge, and deeply hidden inspirations light up like summer fireflies. It often happens for me when I keep my mind occupied by utilizing a type of mantra. For instance, as I plunge my hands into the dark, rich soil, I repeat to myself that weeding the garden is as important as combing my hair. Unknotting the ground ivy and the chickweed from twisting around the bushes and plants is taking care of the earth like I take care of myself. Over and over the rake becomes an extension of my soil-stained fingers as they untangle the weeds and aerate the soil. My body settles into a rhythm that does not need any instructions. There is only silence as I thank the land for allowing me to care for it. My body relaxes in its rhythm, my mind is grateful to be given a respite, and I am more open to inspirations or intuitive feelings as they emerge. These messages can occur in waking moments as well as in nighttime dreams.

Continuous Body Messages

Body messages never go to sleep. Some of my most powerful somatic insights come when I am asleep or in a deep, restful state. Like a knot suddenly released from a tangle of yarn, the symbolic language that surfaces when I relax helps me decipher what is happening in my body.

Most times I remember my dreams. It is my practice to understand them in a way that my brain, replete with overactive thinking, will not have prime authority. I do this by focusing on how my body feels when I awaken or by feeling the emotion that draws my attention to one or two of the dream images. In this way I ensure that the mind is not the only source of interpreting what surfaces from the dream landscape. For example, I recall a particular dream that involved a pilot, a navigator, a spaceship, and a wise old woman. I gave it a title: "An Unearthly Code." I knew that devoting time to this dream would be like getting comforting nourishment from a hot bowl of homemade soup. I needed to swirl the broth around my tongue as if trying to distinguish the ingredients, the spices, and the flavors until there was a final aha moment, when I identified the one zesty detail that tugged at me.

A few of the symbols that pop out for me are navigator, outer space, and code. In my dream I point the pilot toward the stratosphere and tell him to go as fast as he can. There is going to be an explosion—not just any explosion, a nuclear explosion. Big. Life changing. Go, go, go! There is a need to get out of here fast. But once we reach a higher elevation, I asked the question, "What are the ramifications of the explosion and of escaping Earth itself?"

Suddenly, we appear back on Earth. This time I am with a young girl, who is my daughter, as well as the pilot. Under strange circumstances we meet an older wise woman, who takes us to her home. I immediately feel safe. I sense that my daughter and the wise woman recognize each other, and I am where I need to be.

In my dream I have accessed the higher parts of my consciousness. I have played all the roles: pilot, navigator, articulate young girl, and wise woman. I am grounded now, back on Earth. I am home.

Before we go further into my dream, it helps to understand that important images, symbols, icons, or signs are ever present in our lives. It doesn't always have to be a dream that draws our attention and pulls out a symbol for us to contemplate. It could be a wish, a daydream, an inspiration, a thought; these are only a few ways that the Otherworld and prodding from the unconscious beckon us to awaken. Once you recognize a sign or identify a symbol, which may become a repetitive pattern in your thoughts, use that image to move forward in your inner exploration. Don't overthink how or what to do. Ask yourself which symbol or archetype revisits you. Then take a look at what emotions come up, and zero in on where the body feels this sensation.

This is what I did with my dream. Furthermore, I realized that I wanted this to be an embodiment experience and not so much a mental exercise. I felt drawn to finding a way to use my dream and interact with all my senses. To begin this exploration, I centered myself. Generally I find that the early-morning hours provide the best darkened natural light, and the world is quiet and still at rest. I asked myself what happened in my body as I was escaping in the spaceship and then took a pause to step back and examine. Where did I feel it? With eyes closed, I retraced my dream steps and remembered a vibration all over my body. What was the tone and emotion of the vibration? Was it excitement, fear, loud, or gentle? In my dream my breath sped up. My whole torso was involved with this breathing. In the dreamscape my chest was heaving in and out, and there was an added tightness in my throat. My heart felt a pressure as I remembered how I needed to escape Earth. My whole body was pressed back into the navigator's seat with the thrust of acceleration. I felt worried and nervous as I glanced back to Earth and wondered aloud about the ramifications of what was happening. Unexpectedly appearing back on Earth, I felt surprised—not shocked but a kind of extreme wonderment. Perhaps it was confusion about what was going to happen next. However, now my body felt calm amid these extremes.

This dream and my interpretation of it is taking place during the season of Samhain, when the walls between the worlds are thin. It is the time when heightened mindfulness brings special insight. I believe that following, or at least being aware of, the seasonal calendar can provide additional information concerning Earth's energy. For instance, if the moon's gravitational pull creates the ocean tides or if lunar phases affect bird migration, why wouldn't the sun, moon, and stars impact the human species? Knowing that Samhain is a sensitive time of year, with the potential to amplify inner awareness, I revisited the dream again. This time I recalled that there is another aspect of the story to which I circled back at the end of the dream. With the fearful drama over, the first thing that pops into my dream-mind is the code. I've been given a special code, and I needed to decipher it. What is this code, and how am I to crack it? It is this inquiry I bring with me to the embodiment experience.

Assimilating the Meaning

I've gathered resources, books that help me to understand how dream messages are reflected in bodily reactions, how the brain is affected by emotions, and how our belief systems influence biology. They will help me decipher my dream for sure. Books have been my tool to lean on in the past, but this time I am drawing on other methods to get in touch with my senses. This time I will use ceremony, breathing techniques, walks in the woods, and creative expression as my guides. These are the practices that will help with leaning into that place of inner knowing and sacred intelligence.

Here are some of the daily practices that I engaged in my experiment to feel with my body rather than solely use my mind to connect with inner wisdom. First, I have an early morning meditation ritual. For me there is a magical quietness that covers the world like a soft, warm blanket in the cool, gray light of this time of day. Based on my experiences, it is a time when my muse is most active and ready to communicate. Incense fills the air around me as I sit cross-legged on a pillow. Holding my clear quartz pendulum in one hand and my *lia naofa*—the Irish words for sacred stone—in the other, I begin the shamanic drumming or listen to nature sounds on my phone app. Comfortable and quiet on my pillow, I enter the imaginal realm with my sacred circle through meditation. These are inner female/male spirits and animal guides who are with me in my contemplative practice. Together we sit in my prayerful world, and I ask them for help with my dream, with revealing this code. I place that intention in the middle of our circle so we might unravel its meaning. When I do this there is a sense of another presence emerging.

Yoga and deep breathing are a part of my morning routine as well; I practice both after meditation. I immediately feel a vibration throughout my body when I breathe deeply. It is effortless to sense and feel the kundalini energy snaking up and down my spine. It calms me down, creating a sense of groundedness. Yet I'm reminded that a bodily sensation is not the main focus of my meditative exercise rather it is letting my body conduit the meaning of the code symbol in the dream. I patiently wait, remaining open to some insight.

After yoga I go for a walk in the woods. It is my practice to seek the energy among the trees to give me a sign. There is a lineage there, a natural history imprinted on the neighbor-wood that I actively reach out to as I pass through. "I'm here," I say. "I'm grateful I can walk among you in this way." I ask this ancestral ecological energy to help me understand what needs to be known. There is no significant thought concerning my code, however, as I continue my walk. I begin to breathe intentionally and allow my worries to fall away. I want to pay attention to what is currently happening. Circling back to my intention to seek the energy in the woods, I ask what wants to be known. And by utilizing the simple rhythmic motion of walking, I open myself to the contemplation of the moment.

This time, instead of the answer my mind was looking for, I saw what the landscape wanted me to see. Even if its message was purely symbolic, I felt a strong desire to listen. The linear lines of tree trunks and the outstretched branches of tulip poplars showed me their sensual yellow, orange, and green flowers. The ancient magnolia family would be proud! And then I saw circles, not just tall straight lines, but other geometric shapes. The ground was full of two- and three-dimensional objects. How many other dimensions are there that I am not able to see? One branch poked up from a fallen tree and formed a circle of wooden fingers that lightly touched in a meditative prayerful stance. I needed to see beyond the obvious and really, really observe what was all around.

My daily practice began to call on an inner sacred intelligence by gently floating the intention to understand the dream message of the code but not to force or analyze. An unexpected side benefit to my regular ritual heightened my awareness of how well

I was sleeping, even how much water I was drinking. Somehow my physicality took on a complementary importance. How much exercise I got became a part of this journey as well.

Day in and day out I meditated. I exercised. I walked and began to view the world with the very real possibility that the Otherworld existed. I began to comprehend that my body recognized this other presence, but my mind still resisted. So I gardened and cared for the soil. I walked in the neighbor-wood and listened. I paid attention to the responses and needs of my body. The answer to my query came in a contemplative moment when I allowed my mind to rest while expanding my heart's awareness. It was a twinkling of inspiration as my eyes and feet navigated the tree roots that bulged up from the ground along the pathway. Had I not quietened the concerns and burdens of my mind I would have missed it. The inspiration came as gently as the morning sunlight through the dense canopy. The code became a beacon to write a book. This book. As soon as the inspiration came, my heart beat strongly, thumping against my chest wall in anticipation. Goose bumps appeared on my arms, a sure sign that something special was happening.

Simultaneous to the felt excitement surfaced every possible excuse and reason not to do this project. Sure enough, the ego emerged armed with all its protective gear, holding me back and keeping me from making any number of perceived mistakes that it could conjure. These inner-critic voices held me enthralled. I began to avoid my daily routine of meditating and exercising. I stayed up late, preventing me from rising early—which had always been my best time to write. It was hidden from me at first, but I soon realized there were two opposing inner forces at play: my central desire to manifest this book and a fierce protective inner objection to writing it. Thankfully, I eventually understood that objections are sometimes an inner force, planted to protect the story we live by, that is based on the fear of failing. While I bowed in recognition of this fear, I opted to seek a balanced response. In turn, I adopted a new mantra. It became one word: Onward.

The Threshold

There are life phases in which you are aware of being at a threshold, a doorway between the present moment and what is about to happen next. My experiment, born out of a dream and my desire to become more in tune with my gifts of intuitive knowing, brought me to this in-between, liminal space of what is already known and what is yet to emerge. The Otherworld and the unconscious share a language that speaks in images and symbols. Practicing sensitivity to messages from these realms fosters the emergence of signs and synchronicities that are communicated to bring about wholeness, which is the inner wisdom we seek.

To give myself a gift at this time of Samhain, and because my October birthday was near, I allowed myself a connection to my ancestors. I was drawn to express this link with poetry, another type of symbolic language. I wrote a reflection called "My People," letting the words of my ancestors flow through me. These words came to me as a daydream, an ancestral prayer, something that I felt in my body right down to my bones.

My People

My people came from Ireland, the Donovans and the Kanes.
My people left that island for another called Manhattan.
My people loved to learn and stretch their minds.
My people were artists and those who
deeply connected to the land.
The women of my people were always
thinking about the Otherworld.
There came a time when these women shut down.
"Shhh," they'd say, "else someone hear ya
and think you're a weird one."
The women worked hard, but they scarcely showed joy.

Affection came hard to these women who
were more conscious of what
they shouldn't do versus what was their inner guidance.
My people now are those who, stretching beyond what was,
are plowing a road that hasn't seen the like in many a year.

Learning the language of the Otherworld through dream messages, insights, meditation and prayer, connection to the land where you live, or through the empath's gut feelings is an exercise of dreaming into being. In the dreamscape world—either a daydream, a night dream, or a vision—allow your senses to be drawn into meaningful parts of the story narrative. When I reached out to the symbols in my dream, "An Unearthly Code," I felt a reaction in my body. I sensed what was behind the dream image in order to help me decode its meaning.

The keys to teasing out the message of wisdom in the inner landscape are listening, sensing, and feeling. Dreams, body sensations, and emotions are doorways to the Otherworld. They help pry open the unconscious that beckons us to awaken. By embodying a night dream or a poetic vision, we engage our sacred knowledge through a contemplative practice, feel it in our lifeblood, and allow it to sink in. That is the moment we are fundamentally changed by it.

Journey Exercise

Go to a place that sparks inspirations from your soul. It could be an inside location or somewhere in nature. For me it's the woods. You can stand in your backyard. Or open a window, and let the breeze wash over your face. This place may need to be visited multiple times to allow the ego to rest and for your body to resonate. Wherever you are, close your eyes, and focus only on how nature's breath feels on your skin. Once you begin to feel you are in your special place, there is no need to ask any questions. Just allow this other presence to make itself known to you. Enjoy.

Journey Question

If you were to focus on a dream or a wish or a thought, something that could either challenge you or pique your curiosity, what would that be?

Chapter 3

Discovering How We Dream

As a dreamworker, I am a guide who encourages others to look at their dreams so that the messages awaiting them emerge. It's interesting that one of the things I hear occasionally is that "I don't remember my dreams." You're not alone. Dreams sometimes need to be coaxed into memory. Through special laboratory-monitored investigations starting in the 1950s, scientists determined that we typically have four or more dreams per night. They occur during the rapid eye movement, or REM, sleep cycle. Since then, a tremendous amount of research has been done to determine how we sleep, when we dream, and our ability to remember dreams. Take a look at a device worn on your wrist while you sleep to measure your sleep patterns. You will see how many times you enter REM sleep. It is something that the ancients have always known and now there is scientific language to describe what happens. Dreams are waiting for us to discover them.

Jung said, "The dream is the small hidden door in the deepest and most intimate sanctum of the soul." His words remind me of the lyrics from Leonard Cohen's song "Anthem," when he wrote, "Ring the bells that still can ring/Forget your perfect offering/There is a crack, a crack in everything/That's how the light gets in." I believe dreams are one of the best ways to approach the light behind the hidden door while we journey toward inner wisdom.

Tapping into Dreams

There are many ways to tap the dream world to discover what messages are being offered to us. I love to start this conversation from a place of curiosity. Being curious about the signs, symbols, and archetypes of the unconscious and the ancestral memory of the Otherworld is an important first step in remembering dreams. Or you may simply be curious about the dream you know you had last night but forgot the minute you awakened. What matters is that you have some degree of curiosity to begin to crack everything open and let the light in.

Besides the genuine interest in communicating with your inner wisdom, there are some basic, practical ideas used to recall dreams.

Enter sleep with an intention. Whether you want to remember dreams or not, it is a good practice to do a quick survey of your day. What has come up for you during the day, either in your mind or in your body, that needs gratitude or resolution? Focus on one aspect of what you'd like to explore in your personal life, repeating it several times as you would a prayer or a mantra. Relax your body. Start with your toes and slowly move up your legs, torso, shoulders, and head. Inhale that which brings health, and exhale any stress or unneeded energies you want to dispel. Ask the dream-maker, or any other name you give to your inner spirit, for a dream that helps reveal a deeper understanding of your request. Be patient with yourself. You will gain greater appreciation of your inner wisdom's style of communication through time.

Record your dreams. Be ready to reach for your favorite way of logging your dream musings. Some people like to speak into a recording device, others use a journal. Within arm's length of my bed I have a small dream journal with a mechanical pencil clipped to it. The physical sensation of writing, the movement of my hand, helps me reconnect with images that are swimming around inside. I find that the tactile sensation of my fingers gripping a pencil helps my dream recall and keeps me in the space between sleep and wakefulness. I often barely open my eyes when I begin to write. I don't think about writing in complete sentences or worry that what I'm writing makes any sense. If I do begin to think this way, that is an indication I am leaving the sleep realm. I remind myself that I can always fix what I've written later.

Stay in the dream realm. When thoughts of the day's to-do lists or a need to carry out morning ablutions intrude, close your eyes again. Settle back into the pillow, and grab hold of a piece of your dream to bring you back as far as your memory will allow you to go. Ask the dream-maker to help you remember the important bits. Consciously relax your mind and your body again. Feel that you are back in the liminal space between what was and what's next. Allow whatever wants to emerge.

Dreams are not one size fits all. Some of us dream in narratives or stories. I dream this way. Sometimes I can go on for pages in my journal. However, just as often I am only able to recall a small section or scene within the dreamscape. Whatever comes up is fine. Write down what appears without critique. There are dreamers who say they dream primarily in colors or in geometric shapes. Others are reminded of messages they heard or something one of the dream characters said. And what if you find that your pencil draws images instead of writing words? Sketching what you envision may be what is best for you. There are times that I know, or sense, that I've had multiple dreams during the night. Yet the dream-story fades quickly, and I need to ask the dream-maker for help with remembering. It is at that moment, when I'm not quite awake, that an expansion of the night's message appears. This is what I record. Whatever emerges is what goes in the journal. The meaning can be teased apart later. This is a time to simply record.

When you say you don't remember your dreams, perhaps you are looking too hard for a story and not seeing or hearing the message specially designed for you. And by the way, it is not important to do this every day. Recording dreams can be overwhelming if you are a person who receives a lot of messages. You might want to set an intention before you sleep to calm your inner activity and allow yourself to take a break from intrusive signs or images. There is no rule that says you need to listen deeply on a daily basis or record in a way that matches the journeys of other dreamers.

Types of Dreams

When we think of night dreams, there are typically some basic types: standard dreams, recurring dreams, lucid dreams, healing dreams, and nightmares. And remember, we all dream in our own ways. These types are only guidelines. In general, when you begin to recall and make sense of dreams, first look for a connection to your current personal life. Standard dreams tend to reflect our physical well-being, personal worries, or experiences of joy. For many dreamers, the anxieties, fears, or other emotions that arise in these dreams are common themes. In this case it is a good idea to review what is occurring in your daily activity. For example, this kind of dream message could be job related, have something to do with a relationship, or it may be an anxiety shared by the collective, such as how the pandemic affected so many of us. These types of dreams could be in a story format, felt as a physical sensation, an expression of geometric shapes, or an array of colors.

Even the healthiest person will have nightmares. A nightmare can be triggered by scary images from a movie or a book, something you recently experienced, or perhaps medications you are taking. Nightmares are not uncommon with children. When I was a mother of four little ones, I felt it was important to help them feel safe and relaxed before they slept. Even so, there were times of illness or holiday overeating that could produce a nightmare. On the other hand, recurring nightmares could be an indication of something emerging from a memory that needs to be addressed. It will sometimes come back again and again, guiding us to face the fears we are imagining as a monster, for example, until it is seen and discussed while awake. If all dreams offer messages to assist us in our striving toward inner wisdom, then nightmares are especially important as their dramatic format is designed to wake us up and not forget them.

I would like to recognize that nightmares may be born out of extreme, even traumatic life experiences. One dream shared with me was of a mother who tragically and suddenly lost her daughter. For years she had nightmares of someone stealing from her. She would wake up screaming and trying to beat off the thieves. In such incidences, what emerges can be quite difficult. It takes a certain bravery to face the scary imagery that is reflected in the dreamscape. It may require conversations with professionals who can help you navigate this inner labyrinth in order to achieve health and wellness.

I often had nightmares as a child. I always thought, in part, my huge imagination added to my nighttime images. My nightmares were sometimes recurring dreams, ones that repeated often. I clearly recall one particular childhood nightmare. As an adult, I decided to revisit this dream to help resolve an old hurt. You see, even if we haven't had the dream in a long time, we can still use a key dream symbol to write a new story or design a new ending. In this case, I took an aspect of my old recurring dream and created a poem called "The Cedar Closet." I picked the long-ago dream that involved going into the cellar of my family home and confronting a number of dreadful monsters that I knew lurked there. As I reflected on this time in my young life, I knew my nightmare occurred when my father died. His death caused a huge trauma for the family, including me, to resolve. After composing the poem, I reread it and clearly saw the memory had a darker beginning but transformed into another less gloomy end after the creative exercise. By working with a symbol in this old recurring dream, I integrated the fear and changed the outcome that had remained in my memory for such a long time.

33

Katharine Donovan Kane

The Cedar Closet

So many seasons ago my father built a
cedar closet, a small room really.
It was in the cellar where
a black-bellied furnace that drank dark,
murky oil for supper was
just outside the closet door.

Moist cement and dust bundles along
the cellar walls lay undisturbed and mysterious,
like the monster who I thought lived there.
I'd run down the cellar steps, gripped with fear,
into the sweet-smelling closet,
quickly closing the door—shaking, exhaling the breath I held.

Inside the closet old clothes still hung as new
on several rows of thick horizontal dowels
crossing from one side to the next.
A web of memories left behind keeping themselves company.
My eyes, owl-wide, blinked when I pulled
the long string to the light bulb above.

There were shelves along the dark edges—
cubbyholes of Grandma's vases,
Mom's purses, and high-heeled shoes.
On another, a forgotten manual typewriter
and lots of board games,
all quietly waiting to be visited, like a cemetery of stones.

In one of those corners was my father's briefcase,
frozen in time. Waiting—
just like it was before he left with the
angels—ready to grab for work,

all safely clamped together by the vintage lock
on its cracked leather flap.

I sat on the closet floor my father built and
carefully opened his briefcase,
reverently fingering the slightly yellowed papers
with his logo EJK on top.
I read them one by one and
played office, pretending.

One day I stood taller on the cellar steps and saw
the oil-eating monster reborn an efficiency furnace,
dad's refinished workbench, and an art room where
mom spent hours painting portraits.
Sunlight shone through the windows
high up on the cement walls.

And then the cedar closet became a room of treasures
that still held the fragrance of
sweet-smelling memories,
bringing smiles now as I bowed to the angels
who hovered near.
I felt him with me in that pungent space.

Besides the scary nighttime dramas that alert you to
something amiss, there are also lucid dreams, healing dreams,
and precognitive dreams that allow the unconscious to merge
with our awareness in a semiconscious state. Lucid dreaming is
interesting in that you are dreaming and aware you are dreaming
at the same time. This is a less frequent mode but, if you are
a lucid dreamer, you can use this time to create a different
ending to the night narrative that is occurring. It is not unlike
the poem I wrote in my waking time. A symbol I took from
an old dream brought fuller understanding of what came up

from my unconscious and, in turn, brought a healthier personal integration.

In a similar way, healing dreams bring both awareness and peaceful resolution in the night-time story. Upon awakening, there is a sense of completion, that something happened in the dreamscape to bring about a clarification of purpose or meaning. You may experience a problem that you are working on in waking life is finally solved in your dream.

Precognitive dreams are less common. Those who have them awaken with a sense of anticipation about a future event or a deep wisdom about what lies ahead.

Whatever the type of dream, Jung explained that,

> [N]ot all dreams are of equal importance. Even primitives distinguish between "little" and "big" dreams, or, as we might say, "insignificant" and "significant" dreams. Looked at more closely, "little" dreams are the nightly fragments of fantasy coming from the subjective and personal sphere, and their meaning is limited to the affairs of the everyday. That is why such dreams are easily forgotten, just because their validity is restricted to the day-to-day fluctuations of the psychic balance. Significant dreams, on the other hand, are often remembered for a lifetime, and not infrequently prove to be the richest jewel in the treasure-house of psychic experience.

Beyond Nighttime Dreams

Dreams can happen night or day. Besides night dreams there are daydreams, visions, inspirations, and meditations, including the practice of active imagination. All of these are times when important messages from the unconscious and the Otherworld come to us through the language of imagery. It is another important reason to live a life that pays attention to signs and symbols as well as the lessons they offer.

I am a big day dreamer. As an empath, especially as a child who was unaware of my intuitive gift, I would sometimes drift into a type of trance space, conscious yet not fully present, a sort of "zoned-out" place. I first became mindful of my tendency to momentarily refocus my attention when I was in grade school. I remember a day in the third grade when I was particularly distracted. I became fascinated by dust sparkling and floating on rays of afternoon sunlight beaming in the west-facing windows of my Catholic school. The windows stretched from the ledge just above the classroom heaters to near the ceiling. The sun reached across half the rows of students, leaving the others in the shadow. My teacher talked, but I watched the dust. You might say I wasn't a good student because I didn't pay attention, and sometimes I did get in trouble for this habit. Or you could say that as a young student I was simply bored and wished to be somewhere else. Perhaps the best explanation was, as an empath, I occasionally needed to block out the energy of the sixty other students in the overcrowded classroom. There were six rows and ten students per row; I used to count them. I was very aware of who was in the room, where they sat, and their energy emanating from their places in the classroom. I felt the sun's warmth on my face. I had a strong desire to open the window next to my seat to feel the breeze. It slightly rattled the panes, as if to get my attention. Sometimes birds would fly from one tree to the next. I'd wonder about those birds. There was a calm and peace as I imagined being outside with the sun, the afternoon breeze, and the birds. But in less than a few minutes' time, it was over. I woke from the daydream and was back doing an assignment. Yet there was a strong lingering feeling left behind. Daydreams can conjure intuitions or sensations that help us acknowledge niggling thoughts or perhaps give us momentary respite from the overwhelming energy around us.

In addition to daydreams, intuitive inspirations, and creative visions there are ancient spiritual traditions that, when adapted to our contemplative rituals, are helpful in focusing our minds and spirits to gain insight. These practices use repetition of words, intentional breathing, or envisioning exercises to enter an in-between realm, where messages from the unconscious or the Otherworld can safely emerge. Symbols, auditory messages, or strong physical responses from dreams can be used with these practices as well. Traditional observances passed along to us from the ancients are meant to be organic and evolve over time, not maintained as stagnant exercises for their own sake. What makes them time honored is their adaptability to each era. Incorporating a version of these rituals into our own observances connects us to an ancestral lineage that shares its sacred intelligence while helping the tradition grow into a new, more vibrant creation. Here are a few practices and tools that have been meaningful to me.

Mantras and Meditation Beads. Quieting the mind and allowing inner wisdom to be heard can be experienced through repetition. Rosary, misbaha, mala, knotted prayer rope, or Bahá'í prayer beads are a few of the various handheld tools that have their roots in ancient times. The beads are fingered, keeping track of where you are in the prayerful recitation while your mind repeats the mantra. The mantra, a sacred word or sound, is repeated over and over until the vibration and spoken rhythm merges with a person's breath and heartbeat. The mind/heart/body connection come together to ease the busy mental activity and create a safe space for your divine nature to surface.

Centering Prayer and Zazen. Christianity and Buddhist contemplative practices coincide in their spiritualities of interior silence. While their meditative styles derived from different traditions, the practice of relaxing physical movement, refocusing

38

of inner mental chatter, and returning again and again to our personal centers is emphasized.

Fr. Thomas Keating, an American Trappist monk and priest, was one of the principal developers of the practice of centering prayer. Drawing from the Christian contemplative tradition, centering prayer was created as a contemporary meditative tool in 1975. The method begins with an intention to be open and aware of your own inner divine source—or whatever term you use for the true self within—during the exercise. It's that simple. Sit with your back comfortably straight or in a position conducive to your regular meditative practice. Write down or say aloud the prayerful intent you've chosen to focus on. You may decide to hold a stone, a crystal pendulum, or prayer beads. This is only a suggestion. The important aspect is do whatever needs to be done for you to relax in to a meditative pose. Now observe. Practitioners of centering prayer will tell you that almost immediately, our minds throw a multitude of thoughts our way. This sometimes creates stress since we often believe successful meditation is accompanied by an empty mind. However, the emergence of thoughts is normal and is as welcome to be there as our life breaths. When you become aware of thoughts, centering prayer recommends reciting a sacred word or sound that has deep meaning for you as a reset point, bringing you back to a place of inner rest. Simply allow the flow of thoughts to come, and once you become aware of your mind's activity, release whatever has come up. The rhythmic practice of emerging thoughts and releasing without judgment is sometimes met by surges of feelings such as grief, shame, or guilt. These emotions can attach themselves to the thoughts coming up from our unconscious or from our daily concerns. They are not meant to be pushed away or suppressed by some expectations that we have placed on our meditative outcomes. Rather, centering prayer is a healing experience whereby we allow thoughts and emotions to arise without holding on to them. The key is nonattachment.

Here again, like the emerging symbols and archetypes from the unconscious experienced in dreams, the echo of hidden thoughts that arise in the meditative state also want the opportunity to be seen. Seeking the support from a therapist, spiritual director/ companion, or coach may help you to work through more challenging reflections. The image of a spiral for centering prayer helps us to understand that in the process of becoming, or what Jung would call individuation, we meet our inner casts of characters again and again as we cycle through this type of contemplative self-awareness. Each time we become less attached to our stories of limitation and ever closer to our inner true selves.

There are a number of Buddhist traditions with rich spiritual roots, but my experience is specifically with Zen, a Buddhist practice introduced to Japan through China. One of the practices of Zen Buddhism is *zazen,* which means seated meditation. Sitting Zen is a way to get in touch with one's true nature, which is called Buddha nature.

Entering into zazen initially requires attention to posture and breathing. Your whole body is engaged with this experience of inner awareness, so beginning with a focus on somatic alignment is key. A Zen cushion or zafu is helpful so that your knees and lower back are supported correctly. Based on your flexibility and how your knees and legs are folded helps determine what type of cushion to choose and how best to get comfortable. Your back rests in a straight, natural alignment, while your head lifts up from the crown, and your chin is slightly tucked in. The chest is open, and your shoulders are back and down. The mouth is gently closed as the tongue touches the back of the teeth and upper palate to enhance proper breathing. Your arms rest just above your navel, forming a circle as your hands slightly overlap, and your thumbs softly touch. Your eyes are opened a little bit with a downward gaze. The objective is to keep all the senses open and aware. In the same way, your ears are listening without becoming attached to what is being heard. The body's posture supports the flow of breath, which is another key element of zazen. Relax your chest as you breathe, expanding the abdomen in a natural rhythm of inhaling and exhaling through the nose.

As with centering prayer, the practice of zazen is accompanied by the inevitable emergence of thoughts and emotions. These images, ideas, concerns, worries, and other sensations are a part of our true Buddha natures. Therefore, they are to be as welcome as the inner peace that we seek. The challenge is not to become attached to the story that we've built around these thoughts. Zazen encourages us to focus on the rhythm of the breath to bring us back to center by releasing and letting go again and again. The rubrics of getting started with zazen's seated meditation may seem daunting, and truly some people seek a meditation teacher to begin. However, with practice it becomes second nature, and the procedures fall into the background as the heart of the true self comes to light.

While living in Japan in my mid-twenties, I wanted to explore my interest in Eastern religions and practices. I smile at myself now as I remember boldly knocking on the Zen monastery door of a small temple near my home in a northern section of Kyoto. A monk answered and was shocked to see me standing there. I didn't speak much Japanese, nor he English, but we began to use facial expressions and hand gestures to help us communicate. He motioned for me to wait and hurried away, returning with another monk who acted as translator. I explained that I was drawn to their monastery door by the hope that I could meditate with them. I practiced meditation on my own, and what I desired most was to learn how this was experienced in their tradition. I knew this was taking a big risk, yet with bravery born out of my younger self, I sat quietly as the monk contemplated my request. He quickly got up and hurried out of the room as the other monk explained that he would return soon. With much generosity, I was invited to begin the practice of zazen with them, which happened daily in the wee hours of the morning. My early-morning routine quickly adapted to include this Zen practice.

Weeks after starting my predawn zazen I had my first conversation with the temple's Zen master or roshi. In a manner of speaking, the roshi was the abbot for the monks who studied there. He asked why I had come. "Did you want to convert to our tradition?" he wondered. Because if so, he wanted me to know that there was another more widely known temple that catered to Americans. I smiled politely, thanked him, and explained that I had no interest in that kind of training since, for me, converting from one tradition to another wasn't why I was there. Rather, I simply wanted to understand interior silence as experienced in their sacred Zen space. He nodded, and soon the monks began to welcome me to have breakfast with them after morning meditation was over. In the next year I watched, listened, and practiced with the small community of monks. They were my teachers in learning how to pay attention to and quiet my body and mind. I discovered for the first time about physical body alignment and the importance of breath. I began to understand breath as a flow of energy, which is key to overall health and spiritual well-being. In addition, I learned how to accept what came up. And that's the point, isn't it? This practice of mindfulness, or any meditative exercise we chose to do, was another way to create inner and outer places of safety, where intuitions or inspirations can emerge and be heard.

Lectio Divina. This ancient Christian practice is still used in contemplative circles. Roughly translated from Latin, it means "sacred reading." There are four steps to this meditative exercise, but I believe you will easily see the connection to the other practices I've discussed: read, meditate, pray, and contemplate. This method can be applied to any poem, favorite passage from a book, dream, or scripture. To practice lectio divina, a chosen piece is read two or three times, allowing the overall message to sink in deeply and resonate. Breathe rhythmically, and relax the mental chatter until a word, phrase, or image from the reading begins to capture your attention. Next, spend time prayerfully focusing on what the poem or reading has offered you. What has been triggered in your heart? Contemplate what the selected phrase or image is trying to convey. Allow your imagination the freedom to write without restraint or to use another creative way to express what wants to emerge. Poetic imagery or dreams with strongly felt memory content are perfect for the practice of lectio divina. The meditative, concentrated focus helps quiet the mind and opens a portal to sacred intelligence.

Finally, I'd like to briefly mention Jung's technique of *active imagination*. What I'm exploring here is a good, nontherapeutic, Jungian-inspired practice when trying to understand something new arising from a dream or vision. Before beginning the exercise, you may find it helpful to write out a question concerning a character or a memory related to an emotion or somatic reaction when it was experienced in a prior dream. First, slow down the mind and the body through an intentionally relaxed posture and breathing. Begin to bring forth the dream as you remember it. Simply be there in the visualization. While breathing naturally, observe what is happening all around you. Explore the dreamscape, opening your peripheral vision and engaging all your senses to any sound, color, and smell—even any sensations of touch and taste. Allow whatever or whomever wants to make itself known come to you. The purpose here is to release the conscious mind from placing any undue expectations on this meditation. In this practice you sit, wait, and observe. Once a symbol, image, or figure becomes visible, make note of it. No need to do anything or force any resolution. Simply make note of whatever becomes conscious. You can unpack this new information later with your dreamworker or through your self-discovery process.

Learning how we dream is another way of listening to our inner wisdom. As Jung explained, it is like opening a small hidden door to your soul. Tapping into our dreams and visions can be done by following simple steps to prepare and open ourselves to the possibilities awaiting us. Jung echoes the deep-listening practices of the ancients when he said, "Your vision will become clear only when you can look into your own heart."

Journey Exercise

Choose a dream or a dream fragment that you would like to explore. Use this short meditation to reenter your dream for greater clarity.

- Relax your body, and take deep cleansing breaths.
- Settle back into your dream, recalling what you remember seeing and feeling.
- Go back to a place in your dream where you felt the most energy, a place that holds the most power or draws your attention.
- Widen the scope of what you saw before.
- Take in all of what the dream is showing you now.
- Breathe in. Count to three. Then breathe out slowly, counting to six.
- Feel how the dreamscape affects your body. Breathe again intentionally.
- Patiently notice new aspects of the dream, and let them wash over you. Now describe your dream again in your journal.
- What did you see and feel this time that you missed before?

Journey Question

What several images or moments in your dream segment or meditative practice most drew your attention? Describe the images and then contemplate the feelings that emerge. Reflect on how this information may be interpreted given what is going on in your life at the moment.

Chapter 4

Poetry: Wrestling with Nature

WHEN IN COLLEGE I LIVED WITH LEONA, A VIBRANT WOMAN IN her eighties who generously opened her home to young women needing a safe place to live and study. She was a storyteller. Listening to her fascinating tales, she often began by saying, "Tell me if I've told you this before." It took a long time to convince her that even if I heard her adventures before, there was always something new to learn, so I was open to hearing them again.

In an important way, Leona inspired not only my passion for the work I do but taught me to listen deeply to the tales others have to tell. I believe those moments are sacred. I am honored to share someone else's stories, and at the same time, I keep my ear carefully attuned to the hidden messages in-between the words. Leona taught me to become a storyteller's best friend. Wild tales and windswept stories are nourishment to my soul. Tales offer guideposts on the soul's journey homeward. Indulge me, then, as I become the storyteller and speak about moments when I was in tune with my own sacred space and noticed meaningful signs appear.

When introducing myself, I characteristically say that I'm from a family of artists. Truly I am, and I'm proud to be included in the lineage of rich imagination. I love to see what my artistic siblings create: watercolor paintings, pottery, collages, intricate paper cuttings that amaze and delight. Typically they are not far from their tools: brushes, graphite pencils, kneaded erasers, paints, X-ACTO knives, or sculpting loops. My mother was the same way. I have brothers who love to play in the dirt as they mold and shape their outdoor gardens. They will talk with you at length about which grasses are best for what soil or various tree species or the correct plant to put where. They get that knack from our father.

It astounded me, although maybe it shouldn't have, when one day I looked at a dream that I had scribbled down in my journal and envisioned molding it into a poem. In one of those fabulous intuitive bursts, I saw that I had gotten out my tools—my personal resource book of poem structures, my pad of paper, my mechanical pencil, and my laptop. I put in earbuds to listen to recorded nature sounds, soothing the urban noise. I entered my imaginary world, circling around my dream much like a sculptor walks around a piece of raw, uncarved rock. The artist waits patiently for the stone to speak to him or her, asking the stone what form wishes to come forth. In a type of active imagination exercise, I returned to my dream, asking it what poetic form it wanted to take. My goodness! In that moment I saw all of us, my siblings and me, hoisting our respective tools, circling our imaginations, and asking our intuitions to reveal a creative spark. I felt in communion with my family's artistic heritage right in the pit of my stomach. This affirmed that I was asking my dream the right question about how it would best manifest a solid form from its imaginal expression. With this vision, the door to my inner voice opened. My muse smiled at me from the other side of the portal.

I saw the confirmation of my own artistry. It came in the interpretation of a dream as a clear sign and led to the development of my gifts as an empath. When I reentered my dream in the meditative process of writing poetry, I touched the part of my nature called true self or the inner eye. In that moment, several realizations slipped out of my unconscious into awareness. You create images with words, and you have a special empathic connection to nature.

This self-understanding became enchantingly transparent to me on a visit to western North Carolina. Very early one winter morning I recorded a beautiful moment during a walk in the woods. It was a video of geese honking loudly, calling to one another from one side of Kanuga Lake to the other. I wanted something of this magical place to bring home with me. It was just before sunrise, and the early mist lingered enough to cast a wispy blanket over the placid lake. With hardly a ripple across the surface, it was easy to see the watery path of two large geese as they swam across the lake to meet a smaller goose that approached from the other side. They honked and honked, sounding like harbor bells echoing their location. I peeked at them from behind the cover of trees and sparsely leaved bushes as I listened to their back-and-forth refrain. Except for the geese, I was alone in this experience. I imagined myself as a fairy who slipped to the surface from the underworld through the roots of the nearby tree. And like all fairies, I was careful to stay hidden. My fingers steadied the iPhone camera. I pressed the video button to record. Keeping my breath slow and even, I waited. Something was about to happen. But what? *Patience, I* thought. *Be still.* Would the approaching geese fight, or would they be happy to reach each other? What do geese do when they're alone on a lake with only the wood fairies watching? Finally, they reunited and merged into one unit, one family. As if in a dance they turned in a synchronized circle to swim in one direction—together. Now I knew.

I felt like I was given a secret and was inspired to write a poem to express it. Creating a poem about an experience is one approach to bring the story alive in a deeper way. Challenging ourselves to engage the language of symbols and metaphors cracks open a new means of using our senses and being attentive to the here and now. I love haikus and how they capture nature reflected in a momentary flash of time. A poetic structure of three lines with five-seven-five syllables respectively is both simple and inspired.

I decided that I wanted to string together a triplet of haikus into one poem. Here is what came about.

Kanuga Lake, North Carolina

Evoking a Dance

The fairy watches
milky mist kiss placid lake.
Honking geese arouse

the landscape within.
Shadows of dawn reach morning,
calling. Evoking

a dance. Vibrating,
anticipating, she stirs.
His song awakens.

An October Surprise

In Takoma Park, Maryland, where the trees near Long Branch Creek were transitioning into autumn, I saw nature's fireworks of color celebrating the change of season. Gardens exploded in the merry pumpkin shades of marigolds and in the deep maroon of the red maple trees. At once there was a beautiful palette of green, lime, yellows, and cherry reds. It was on one of these days when visiting a friend I found myself awakening to this canvas. I didn't have to move; I opened my eyes, and there it was. Deep within my gut I felt an urgency to get up and write. I quickly wrote down my dream fragments and felt the dim morning light was a perfect time to create a poem inspired by the dream. With pencil and writing pad close by, I was ready to go. I had everything I needed for composing, I thought, including the quiet. I waited and waited for inspiration. Apparently she was still sleeping. Nothing was coming. In general, I am not easily deterred. Nor was I this time. I know how to arm wrestle with my muse if I need to! Chiseling away at the dream with my words, I was hopeful that the right inspiration would show itself.

Out of this struggle came the unexpected call of a distant owl. An owl? I hadn't heard one here before in the surrounding woods. My distracted thoughts began to wonder, *Why haven't I heard an owl before?* I knew that they were there, as well as hawks, because at sunrise, the crows cawing told me so. There it was again. The owl. This time a lot closer. I was fully listening now. And then it happened: a poem. Not from the dream I had chosen but one about the owl. What could I say about this owl that hadn't been composed before? *Who cares about that?* my muse responded to me.

Sometimes a poem catches us by surprise. This one did. I didn't try to control it; I allowed myself to become a metaphorical vehicle for what needed to emerge. I began to write; this time the words came easily. This is what I wrote that morning to my muse and to my owl:

Dawn

At dawn
  I heard it.
    My ears remembering,
      they perked up
at the sound
  of the owl's hoot
    to call me
      out of sleep.
I'm here, I say;
  awake, I listen,
    wondering about messages
      from dark night places.
Window propped open
  to the touch of morning's moist,
    clean breath.
      I'm here, I say.
Where are you?
  Don't go yet.
    I want to know the mysteries
      from dark night places.
I promise to stay
  awake this time,
    anticipating, quiet
      like the darkness before birth.
And then it's sunrise.
  Owl hidden now—again.
    Other birds chirp, crows caw,
      filling the world with their racket.
Awake, I listen.
  I'm here, I say.
    Let's meet again
      at dawn.

Dream Flow

I remember another time when I was determined to create a poem from a dream. I wanted to take a dream and see if the process of crafting a poem told me something I needed to know. Like the surprising appearance of the owl in my poem "Dawn," I intended to explore more about what was hidden in the dark places of my personal unconscious, a womb space awaiting the birth of awareness.

Most often I dream in narrative. I am surprised when there isn't some kind of story line. This is just the way it happens with me. However, there are dreams that come in vignettes or even one-line messages. My dreamscape knows what I love. It knows that I appreciate a good tale. One night a dream came in which I was in Ireland. I was near my current age, and being in Ireland seemed ordinary. In the dream I appeared to be an observer as well as a participant. I noticed stone-like figures, a wise woman and children. I was confused by what the stone figures were looking at, but I felt happy with the wise woman. When I awoke, I focused on the key symbolic elements of the dream story and on the strongest emotional pull of its message. I chiseled out a villanelle, a type of French poem popular in the nineteenth century, by remembering what happened in the dream and creating a poetic silhouette to see what message would emerge. Here is what I wrote:

The Storyteller

I met the Storyteller with magical eyes.
My heart connected with her from ancient time.
She looked deeply and smiled at my surprise.

I first came during Imbolc, as winter dies.
Robed men like statues stood, pretending divine.
I watched the Storyteller's magical eyes.

A knowing, a blessing, an enchantment flies.
My breath holds; she weaves a tale, a soothing rhyme.
She looked and smiled again at my surprise.

The page turned. Where statues were, children arise.
There's a light now; the breeze catches a wind chime.
I see the Seanchaí with magical eyes.

"It's me," I say. "Have you not heard my cries?
I'm magic, a unicorn, a dragon, I'm ..."
She looked deeply and smiled at my surprise.

I stopped, slowly exhaled my life in disguise.
I had finally come back, roots sprouted this time.
I met the Storyteller with magical eyes.
She looked deeply and, imagine my surprise!

Once Upon a Journey

Inis Mór. How could I not have moments out of time on this
Aran island off the West Coast of Ireland? It seemed like a deluge
of ancestral memory and emotions during my early-spring visit.
There was a tug to that place. The long walks. The conversations
I'll never forget. Was it poetry or prose I wrote or both? I didn't
matter; I let the words come. There was an outpouring of poem
after free-form poem. Sometimes it's like that. Using personal
experiences as a starting point to break open the unconscious is a
profound place to start. I hoped that somewhere in the jumble of
words that came to me on Inis Mór was what I needed to hear.
Here is what I wrote, some photography that I captured, and a
little of what I learned from allowing myself to be the conduit for
the messages that emerged.

Wrestling with Nature

I am in a wrestling match with myself,
so I go to the sea.
I am here, but my home is on the other side of it.

The secluded Aran island beach on a chilly dawn
draws my inner guide near.
At the very least she should be!

A cool shiver from the wet sand
seeps into my bare feet
as I watch the drama of night turn into dawn.

My eyes squint to see the eastward hills.
I catch a rippling light, then shadows,
then yellowish frosting on the tips of the waves.

The inlet doesn't ask; it just welcomes my
presence as it receives the sunrise.
It's not comparing itself to the larger ocean around the bend.

Grappling with itself, the sky weaves deep
blues splashed with slivers of gray,
entwining together in a dance showing me how it's done.

I go to the sea and find the intense beauty of outstretched arms.
Her cool morning offered a warm embrace
instead of the wrestling match.

Earth's Language

I'm standing in an undisturbed field of high green grasses.
The isle breeze pushes each blade as it flutters and sparkles.
Birds feel safe to call from the next tree or bush.
So many voices.

I'm standing amongst it all, journal in hand.
My pencil floats across the page like a wood white butterfly.
Welcomed in this meadow, I reverently observe.
If I sit would I make too much noise?

I'm standing while the gentle wind sings a lilting song
as it passes through the iron cow fence nearby.
The insects buzz, and the birds sing along, and
waving, waving the grass continues to dance.

I'm standing as a large bee flies close and startles my attention.
It watches me closely guarding this simple patch of beauty.
There's a mew call from the gulls attracting me to the sea.
Time to go.

Primal Essence

A spring rain beating on the
freshly unfurled leaves,
the aroma of wet, lush soil.

Whisperings within begin
an awakening from dreams;
woodpecker tapping on dead wood, calling.

Ancestral heart freed by deep listening,
beating with primal flow—come,
and you're truly welcome by the hearth.

Stone Etching

Stone etching welcomes
Misting from selkies haven.
Ancient rebirthing.

As an empath, I have gut feelings. I sense the energy of people and animals and feel the vibration of the earth that surrounds me. When in Ireland, I become acutely aware that I am walking on the same land of my ancestors, and because of this, I feel physically connected to their stories. The last time I visited I made a conscious decision not to question my gift anymore. I learned to give it full permission to speak through my unique voice as a highly sensitive empath who is compelled to write and create whatever comes from it.

We all have something in common. That is, through our dreams, experiences, memories, and inspirations, we hold the opportunity to apply the language of symbols and metaphors to write poetry or give the unconscious and the Otherworld another way to communicate with us. Be open, enter the liminal space of waking dream time, and allow the inspiration to come.

Journey Exercise

If you are fortunate enough to walk the land from where your ancestors came, that's wonderful. But it's not necessary. You can still be in touch with ancestors. Where are you now? Close your eyes. Sit on the ground or touch a tree. Breathe deeply, and feel the damp, cool hardness of the earth. Let the breeze reach over and touch your face. There are people who once walked that land. Allow yourself to take in everything about where you are.

Journey Question

From where you are sitting now, the land, the trees, and the animals are telling stories. Focus on one element of nature. How are you sensing it, feeling it, or hearing it? How is connecting to it impacting you in the present moment?

Chapter 5

Envisioning the Soul

I was sitting in Señor Solar's Spanish class in junior high school. I loved his class, though I didn't think I was good at languages. What I loved was his way of teaching. For me, Spanish class was like being in a philosophy class, which I learned I had an affinity for in ninth grade. One day as Señor Solar was explaining something, I raised my hand. When he called on me, I started my question with, "I wonder." I am not sure I got the rest of the question out because he stopped me and said, "That is one thing that I appreciate about you." I must have looked something in between embarrassed and stunned because he continued by saying, "You wonder. That is what we should be doing in school … wondering."

Again I find myself wondering. I am deeply curious to know what inner wisdom looks like. As a life coach and dream facilitator, I've spent time learning the language of symbols and images, which is the way dreams and the inner self communicates with us. I suppose you could say that I am good at languages after all. The seeds of awareness about the archetypal unconscious and the imaginal Otherworld starts with the curious intention to understand. The idea of our inner wisdom begins to make sense when it is exhibited in tangible form, such as a visible sign that confirms our intuitive experience. I use inner wisdom and sacred intelligence interchangeably since for me they both signify our core essences. "Sacred" is an important word describing the holy ground of true self, the place where there is a concrete expression of our understanding of the divine.

My curiosity has tapped into this common thread we all share. I have a need to know what stirs deep within us, a place where human consciousness becomes divinity.

Geometric Art Forms

Mandalas are a sacred art form that originated around the fourth century AD in places like Tibet, Nepal, China, and Japan where Buddhism blossomed. A mandala is a visual manifestation of a meditative state of being. In the Sanskrit language, "mandala" means circle, an enclosed container in which the Self, or true self, has a safe space to express itself in symbols, colors, and designs. This art expression gives an artistic shape to the mental state of being when it's created. Designing, drawing, and coloring mandalas is a healing practice used to help us enter our inner space of in-betweenness of what we are currently experiencing and our capacities to embody it.

Have you ever focused on a creative project so completely that your hands seemed to operate on autopilot, without being controlled by your mind? It doesn't matter if you are cooking, gardening, building, taking photographs, or using art tools. Whatever you are doing, your mind is no longer running the show. Instead, you are lost in a trance, a state of absorption. What comes up in your creative endeavor is the language of shapes and colors and patterns that are there inside you, ready to emerge. Whether your inspired undertaking is a hobby or you are making a sophisticated mandala, channeling your creative energy builds your confidence as an empath.

Jung believed, "The mandala is an archetypal image whose occurrence is attested throughout the ages. It signifies the wholeness of the Self. This circular image represents the wholeness of the psychic ground or, to put it in mythic terms, the divinity incarnate in man."

**Without thinking of creating a predetermined
design, I opened to my inner self, and a
circle of shapes and colors emerged.**

My first attempt at a mandala represented the wholeness or the scattered nature of my inner self at the time. Before I began this exercise, I set paper and my box of colored pencils and markers on the table in front of me. I drew a large circle on the paper and thought about the empty space. I knew that I would put something inside this emptiness, but first I needed to approach my own inner circle to see what wanted to be uncovered. To do this I meditated.

Entering the space where I connect with my inner true self, I relaxed and breathed deeply to quiet the mind and give permission to my body to feel. This type of meditation is like an active imagination exercise. I walk from where I am in my mind's eye into the forest along a rocky pathway that descends and rises again.

There are times I am barefoot and times I have on protective boots. There is a ground-level mist. I pass through it until I reach a grassy area where my spirit-sisters wait for me in a circle. There is always water running in the background. Occasionally it appears as a gentle brook, while in other meditations it is a steadily moving stream. Going to this place before I begin any visualization practice allows me to awaken all aspects of myself I am familiar with while knowing that just beyond the circle are parts of me yet unknown. I am aware that it's all there as I try to open my heart, mind, and body to their fullness. I observe and wait for something to unveil itself.

I began to sketch within the mandala's empty circle. I used simple paper and colored pencils. Nothing elaborate. If I were a Buddhist monk, I may spend hours perhaps days bent over an intricate design using colorful sand to express my inner state of being. My mandala exercise had no agenda, only curiosity to see what I would do if the pencils drew without a predetermined plan. What came up was an interesting assortment of shapes and colors.

The creation of the mandala is one step of the inner journey; it shows us the opportunity to reveal another layer. I took my simple drawing into a second meditation and contemplated what patterns had appeared within the circle. Like the dreamwork we have discussed, the mandala language speaks in symbolic designs to help us learn what we feel or sense about ourselves. I made note of any emotions or bodily sensations that came up and recorded this for later.

Take a look at your design. You may have used an assortment of red, orange, yellow, green, blue, violet or no color at all. Ask yourself about your colors. Did you experience intensity or a tranquil, relaxed association? Were there angular sharp edges to the shapes you used or circular spiral patterns? My mandala showed a number of spiral patterns like mini-labyrinths. I interpreted this labyrinth symbol as a map of my active transformational journey.

There were starlike leaves, too, which I decided to put aside for another meditative journey. For colors I mostly used violet, blue, and green, except for one area at the base of the spiral figure where I used red. I felt that these colors reflected an awareness and harmony in my current life with aspects showing creative tension and strong, passionate energy. I found that I recognized myself in the geometric design within the circle, and it seemed to fit with what was circulating in me at the time.

A mandala is only a snapshot in time. My design—your design—changes each time we enter this unique meditative experience. This exercise is worth repeating again and again.

Like the mandala, circles appear in other ancient representations, such as the Mayan sun design symbolizing enlightenment. The Ojibwe, whose traditional homeland is around the Great Lakes region of North America, originated the dream catcher with its circular hoop surrounding a web of fibers to help filter bad dreams. The Hopi, from Arizona and surrounding southwestern region of the United States, offer us the Hopi spiral that displays separate strands flowing in a curved pattern from the central core. There are architectural creations such as stone circles that appear throughout the northwest coast of Europe, the Gobi Desert in China, and in Africa. I find myself drawn to these sacred standing stones erected on various continents because they express a deep collective energy. Unlike the mandala that typically conveys an individual's inner sanctum, stone circles are art forms that express the inner wisdom of a cultural community. I have had the opportunity to visit some of these places in Central America and northern Europe. A sense of reverence is felt as you walk in the place where ancient peoples have left their sacred intelligence. For empaths and highly sensitive people, these are places that draw out our gifts and bring them to the surface.

Jung introduced the idea of the mandala's sacred expression through a psychological lens to the Western world. For him, the mandala represented an expression of wholeness, an opportunity to characterize all the dissociated parts of ourselves into one integrated balance. It is an artistic representation of what our psyches look like at a particular moment in time. Yet I continued to wonder, *What types of modern mandala expressions are available to us? Are there other artistic motifs that help our inner wisdom slip through a portal from the unconscious to provide us with guideposts along life's labyrinth?*

Nature's Way

Being an earth empath, I am a nature lover. Being outdoors getting my hands dirty playing in the garden or walking along a wooded path is as important to me as the nourishment of good food. It is not uncommon for me to hear birds at a distance and turn their way to see what is happening. I stop along my walks and stare into the woods in a brief trance, trying to imagine what may have been there many years before. It is more than an intellectual reflection about what I am seeing. It is, rather, a knowing or sensing.

One morning many years ago during a vacation, when my children were very young, I stopped at a gas station in the state of Virginia. We all got out to stretch while the mechanic looked at the car's brakes, which were not functioning correctly. The man helping us was friendly and took the time to explain the history of the land around his business. He said that we were standing on ground that was once a field of a big Civil War battle. Curious now, we walked around to the back of the station and stood gazing. There was a huge, green sweep of rolling hills with scattered hickory and red cedar trees. The morning's misty air touched the ground. I asked my girls, "Do you feel that? Do you feel all the activity here?" We all stood quietly. I stared at the place where scores of lives were lost long ago. I sensed them. I felt it deep within my bones. In those days, I tucked away that strong vibrational sensation since, I reasoned, who would believe me? It took me time, but eventually I learned to admit that I have a way of feeling the land.

This story reminds me of something that John O'Donohue, Irish poet and philosopher, once said about how we choose to show up in our lives. He said each time you leave your home you need to decide, "whether you believe you are walking into a dead geographic location, which is used to get to a destination, or whether you're emerging out into a landscape that is just as much, if not more, alive as you but in a totally different form." When I first heard him speak these words, I felt a click inside me. *Yes, I* thought, *the land is just as alive with memory and intelligence as I am.* I knew this because I felt it.

The trees and bushes, flowers, and wooded pathways display a beautiful natural canvas. They are not there merely for our visual enjoyment as if we owned them. Nature provides a sacred space and has its own vibrational energy that communicates messages all the time. To be aware of those messages, we must intentionally decide to interact with this reality just like we do with dreams or with the ancestral memory of the Otherworld.

Ways of Seeing

I regularly take my iPhone camera when I go walking in nature. I always begin by breathing deeply, soulfully honoring the place where I am, and by offering an intention. I ask the woods to reveal what it wants me to learn that day. Posing this question to the landscape is done with a reverence that recognizes I am only one part of the whole. There is a promise underlining the intention that I will use the photographs I take as a focal point in future meditations. I appeal to nature for wisdom to come forward. Like Jung's active imagination dream exercise, I go into the woods, observe, and wait. I allow myself to be drawn into another reality of sorts, a mystery that only the trees and the woodland animals witness.

You can sense a vigorous energy emanating from these images. The way the trees lean on each other suggests an interplay. The light and shadows create beauty that evokes a feeling. The elder trees reach out to the younger ones as if inviting them to grow. If you focus on the photo meditatively, you begin to see deep into the woods. You can almost imagine yourself walking into the trees and being present among them. Standing with the trees and the wildlife gives you a sense that even in the stillness of that one moment there is mystical energy.

Later, when you are contemplating the photograph, remember to let go of the intellectual analysis of the photo's composition. Thinking logically about photographs is a bit like your brain bringing you out of the dream state as it begins to analyze. Instead, when you envision a photograph, enter the woods, and allow yourself simply to observe. Ask yourself what you are feeling, not what you are thinking. What intuitive images pop up for you?

Once you've reached the sensory state, try to stay in it. You can ask yourself later about the meaning.

I mentioned previously the existence of thin places, physical locations on Earth where spiritual awareness is heightened. When you are in one of these settings, you will find yourself pausing from activity. You look around almost as if you heard your name called but are not sure who spoke. Thin places are thought to be holy ground. Or it may be a locale where the Otherworld, the world of the unseen, becomes easily apparent. A feeling, a thought, goose bumps, or a cold shiver overcomes you. Your brain may not process a clear understanding, but there is a tangible reaction. I have experienced places like this.

I would like to suggest, however, there are other global sites without this special thin place distinction that bring us the same intimate interactions with the land. Was there ever a time when the heat or cold on your face was such that it made you touch your cheek and remark how it felt? If believing the wind is nature's breath, then inhale the fresh air. Let it expand in your chest, and allow it to give you a sense of soul medicine. What about the quick changes of sun to rain, or when heavy dark-gray clouds on a cold winter's day open to release sheets of snow crystals. Close your eyes and ask yourself how it feels.

Even if you live in a place where there are not large trees to walk among, the elements of nature still make themselves known. We are given messages all the time. For instance, does your chest clench a little when you look up and see that nature has given you an artistic skyward composition to behold? In my *Lunar Energy* photo, the clouds make me think they take the form of powerful mountains wrapping themselves around the fullness of the moon. The moon reaches out to the darkened trees standing as night guards that watch as moon's vitality pours out from herself onto the world, restoring us while we sleep.

Ask yourself, "What do I see in the nighttime landscape?" If you were to sit quietly with this photograph, what begins to emerge?

Lunar Energy

In the photo *Healing Moon,* the dark night reveals a circular hazy moon that to me is both robust and ladened. There seems to be a network of branches, a dark matrix of capillaries absorbing the energy from the nucleus of her moonlight, bringing it back to the earth. It is nature's lifeline, pulsing heart-energy out to those who would walk on the land below.

Healing Moon

This brings up another question about which I wonder. What if your eyes don't allow you to see what I have shown you here? Does nature have a message for those who sense her in other ways?

I have a story to tell you about my mother, Madelaine. She was an artist and blind in the latter part of her life. However, for most of her life she enjoyed near-perfect vision. She spent a lot of time in her home studio painting portraits of her children or replicating her version of startlingly intense magazine photography. My sensory memory easily recalls the aroma of oil paints and acrylics. I see paintbrushes of all shapes and sizes carefully cleaned with turpentine standing together in a large container. Her artist tools helped set her imagination free. Later in life, as she began to lose her sight, instead of brilliant portraits she painted landscapes that were big washes of bold, dramatic watercolors. The trees and rivers and open spaces from her imagination were not always proportional or perfectly formed, but nonetheless, they pulled you into her inspired genius. After the blindness took over, she used her hands to create pottery, and it became her passion. She felt how the bowl was forming. She would intuit the shape, the texture, and even the color. Laughing with joy at all of it, my mother allowed the vibrational interaction between her hands and the clay to form what wanted to emerge.

As an earth empath, I can understand how this vibrational energy works in the artist's mind. Walking among the trees, sometimes barefoot, and feeling the rhythmic heartbeat of the land, intuiting the memory of the ancestral rocks and trees, and sensing there is an Otherworld. Allowing this life energy to penetrate our reality requires we use a part of ourselves we do not typically access. The land is asking us to use our metaphorical "hands" as well as our "eyes" to understand. It is another way that our sixth senses use our bodies to know or intuit its presence.

Envision with Different Eyes

Our shared inner wisdom sends us messages from the unconscious, nature, or our dream worlds. This indwelling wisdom energy has been given different names in various spiritual traditions. They include Sophia, Shekinah, or Shakti. She has manifested as a goddess, an intricate mandala design, or as ancient geometric stone circles. There are ways that she has yet to be known. What is evident is that she is a communicator who, regardless of how often we miss her signals and how often we mistreat her, she never stops caring or giving. Her favorite language includes signs and symbols. This language does not always make sense to the intellect. She prefers to make herself known through feelings and sensations or moments of intuitive insight.

Inner wisdom also manifests herself in special people in our lives. These are people who call out to us and reflect the gifts we hold. They tell us about the importance of our curiosity and wonderment like my ninth-grade teacher did for me. They are often in plain sight. It may take years to discern the meaning of their insights, yet the synchronicity of their presence may spark us in the moment. My daughter Erin has this type of synchronistic knowing. Periodically she will contact me and begin to call out the gifts she sees in me by telling a story or asking a question. For example, years ago when moving back to the United States after a long-term job in South Central Asia she asked me to help her set up a session with a breathwork facilitator. She was confident that I knew who to call and was equally comfortable that there was no explanation necessary. I would understand what she needed and why. Another time we were chatting online with several other people. As we all discussed possibilities for a new business venture, Erin said, "All we have to do now is to have my mom manifest this idea, and it will happen." This made me smile. Erin has a gift that calls forth the truth she sees in other people or in the formulation of ideas. She speaks the truth that she sees, says it aloud, and gives it a voice. Here again, through the gifts of others, inner wisdom makes herself known.

Journey Exercise

Start with a deep breath before beginning either a nature walk or gazing skyward. Ask wisdom to show you what she wants to communicate. The key is to enter a state of deep curiosity. Keep breathing and then observe and wait—without analyzing.

Journey Question

What is it that has come up for you in this meditative exercise? Did you notice a sign, symbol, or intuit a gut feeling? How does this new insight change who you are in this moment?

Chapter 6

Synchronicities: Seeing with the Inner Eye

"IT's A SIGN." MY CHILDREN WILL ATTEST THEY HAVE HEARD ME express this more than a few times. When I said, "sign," I grouped any number of unusual circumstances together. In some cases, though, what really happened was not a random sign but rather synchronicity, a coming together of events hard to explain why or how it happened but gave us pause. Jung wrote that synchronicity is a "meaningful coincidence or equivalence of a psychic and a physical state that have no causal relationship to one another." He explains that this is no chance meeting but "an unconscious image comes into consciousness either directly or indirectly in the form of a dream, idea, or premonition [and] an objective situation coincides with this content."

Synchronicity is a way of seeing with the inner eye. It is a moment in time when two energies merge: the presence of our inner wisdom with an encounter. In turn, it sparks a deeper understanding of what we are experiencing. It is an aha moment. This intersection can come and go in a flash. Or it can stay with us awhile. It is important to note that synchronism is available to anyone.

I have had a number of these co-instances, some obvious and some so instantaneous that there's hardly any time to recognize it ever happened. One such time was the week my mother was dying. She had a long and beautifully meaningful life. At the time of her passing, she held on until all her far-flung children came to town. Her deepest desire was to see all ten of us together once again. Hospice care workers say it is common for the dying to hold onto life by attaching to a person or one last act.

My daughter Colleen volunteered to stay with my mother through the night at the health-care facility so that someone was with her at all times. Colleen reasoned that being in medical school, she was used to staying up through the night. Very early one morning, when it was still dark and quiet, I unexpectedly awoke. I left the bedroom and sat on the living room couch. I felt my mother. My stomach ached, and there was sadness in the air. I felt a strong urge to be with Colleen at my mother's bedside. I immediately got up to dress when the phone I was holding rang. She said, "Mom, I think you should come." Indeed, my mother had just passed, but Colleen stood guard, keeping the energy of her last moments alive until we all—one by one—came to bid my mother goodbye. Eventually I realized I was so attuned to my mother's energy that I felt a shift when her spirit was leaving us. That shift woke me, and at the same instant I thought of Colleen and my mother, I received a call.

In a similar moment a year or so later, my mother returned the favor to Colleen. Colleen had stayed awake for long hours studying for an exam and then fell into a deep sleep. Her grandmother appeared in Colleen's dream and told her in an urgent voice to wake up! She was jolted awake. And yes, she arrived just in time to the test site, still in her pajamas but ready to take the exam.

Synchronicity for the Eyes That See

Another interpretation of synchronicities is co-creative moments with nature. These moments arise when we are in deep connection to our inner selves. We may prayerfully contemplate a desire or pose a question to the universal spirit. At the same time, we are aware of a special aliveness in the environment around us. Be ready. It is my experience that prayers are answered in ways that match the moods of our queries, such as an oncoming thunderstorm or a magical break in the clouds with unexpected sunshine. This natural event triggers our intuitions, enabling resolutions. It may come as an obvious, direct response to our entreating mantra prompted by the sudden appearance of an animal with special meaning for us, such as a red fox, a large black snake, or the song of a cardinal. Always, though, synchronicity comes wrapped as a meaningful coincidental gift. You can build awareness of this kind of moment by the practice of mindfully entering your sacred inner space and being open to seeing signs repeated in nature. It helps to develop a genuine sense that the world around us has a life of its own with an inherited blueprint that continuously expresses itself.

A mentor told me that once you are aware of synchronicity, you will notice it happening on a regular basis. This has been true for me. I became increasingly conscious of it as I spent more time in prayerful reflection or taking intentional silent walks in the woods. The quandary that has arisen for me in this introspection is this: How do you begin to trust the intuitive messages offered by nature and those emanating from the core of our true selves when you're experiencing it? Trust is important to the empath. Many times there is doubt about the felt vibrational sensations, the sudden inklings of discomfort, or gut reactions when we receive intuitive information about a situation. I am encouraged when I remember the meditative process of becoming aware of my skeptical thoughts and releasing them. Each time returning to my grounded center to give my true inner self a chance to respond and trust the new insights wanting to emerge.

Nothing has been as foundational to my full comprehension of dreamwork and certainly my understanding of being rooted to nature with its essential characteristics as synchronicity. One of

Jung's oft-quoted thoughts fits perfectly here: "Synchronicity is the ever-present reality for those who have eyes to see."

I have a good friend, Ron, with whom I share photography and writing. In learning more about each other at a deeper, significant level we have had a number of synchronistic experiences. One evening I sat on the roof patio of my apartment building. I was thinking about synchronicity, its meaning, and if it is truly possible to be connected to nature as a real and spiritual presence. I looked at the sky and noticed how utterly beautiful it was. I stopped thinking for a minute and simply stared at the evening's early stars.

Early Evening Star

I took the picture *Early Evening Star* and sent it to him. I remember sitting on a bench staring upward when the email response came. Given that he had no knowledge of my musings, I was taken with surprise at his answer. He said, "I like the glowing object, the haze around it makes it look like a painting, or is it a hole in the fabric letting the light in?"

My point in sending the photograph was only that the sky was so beautiful in its precision, and the almost-full moon was so prominent in the evening sky. It looked striking yet plain and simple. Photography is just that for me—a plain and simple break from all my thoughts. The "hole in the fabric" comment, however, startled me. It made me take another long look at what I had seen in the sky. In fact, it did look like a hole and that something was indeed communicating itself. I was intrigued by the coincidence of his thoughts that this photograph captured a portal. It made me think that there is another reality right there with us, trying to come in and show itself.

To me this was synchronicity. It was a direct answer to my reflections that pondered the real and living spiritual presence in nature as a way of seeing the contiguous Otherworld. This experience was what Jung meant as a coming together of my inner state of being with an outer event in a way that was meaningful in the moment but hard to explain. At one time I would have described this interaction as a coincidence worthy of only a momentary thought. I didn't always recognize how precious those moments can be. I am grateful I didn't ignore the message this time.

Another Meaningful Coincidence

Synchronicities or meaningful coincidences are not merely a chance meeting. There is something that reflects a greater dynamic happening. Another story illustrates this.

One day I was walking in a nearby park. I often take these walks and quietly ask the natural world to tell me what it wants me to know or what it wants me to see. I love taking photographs of nature. Water seems to draw my attention the most. This day I was walking along Rock Creek in Washington DC, hoping to capture the way the water sparkled as it tripped over large rocks. Yet every time I went to take a photograph, my shadow intruded in the frame. I chuckled to myself because, of course, shadow work was the latest topic I was concentrating on in my dreamwork studies.

So I gave in and took the picture of my reflection. I called it *My Shadow Self*. Then I clicked the photo and sent it to Ron. I received a reply in the form of a poem he had written months before. I was drawn to a particular section of his writing, so I wrote back, "I was thinking about your last line that said, 'some ideas before its time, searching for the fissure in everything that lets the warmth in, and around.'" That poetic line caused me to look at my image again. I was astonished to see the fissure!

My Shadow Self

In taking the photograph I was only looking at the outline of my shadow; I didn't look inside the darkened figure. I started to piece together what I was thinking as I walked around that very sunny day. Now I saw in my photographic shadow the answer to my request for nature to show me what it wants me to know. I was stunned to see a fissure from the crown chakra all the way to my heart chakra. And as my friend saw, there was something growing from my heart center. Both my hands seemed to be clutching my heart, yet it was me holding the camera. The camera, a metaphor for my inner eyes, was showing me that there was growth happening. The photography and poetry combined to help me see the intersection of my inner wisdom and my outer experience. My friend's astute eye and sharing his poetic writing, the photograph, and my purposeful questioning of nature had created a meaningful coincidence.

Noticing, Seeing, and Trusting

How do you notice synchronicities, and what are we looking for? And more important, how do you begin to trust what you are seeing? For me, the answer is in my own philosophy of taking photographs: It's plain and simple. The energy of contemplative thoughts sends a message, the camera sees, and the creative expression or symbol in the photograph is the universe's reply. First, it is the practice of trusting that indeed a reply will come, noticing what is already there, and then letting it fully blossom in our consciousnesses.

The true self that still rests hidden in the inner realm uses the language of archetypal patterns to help heal life's entanglements through intuitive knowings and dreams. There are any number of definitions of archetypes. When I speak of them, I am referencing the universal and primal images in both mythology and psychology. What makes the mythic story so powerful is that there exists a theme that relates to common human experiences. Some of these motifs are characters such as hero/heroine, villain, trickster, and teachers. Additionally, there are themes such as journeys, life, death, rebirth, upper world, lower world, as well as creation and destruction. Jung influenced the field of psychology by creating a bridge between the primal nature of human experience exemplified in mythic stories to what he calls the collective unconscious. He said, "The collective unconscious consists of the sum of the instincts and their correlates, the archetypes. Just as everybody possesses instincts, so he also possesses a stock of archetypal images."

If I look back over recorded dreams in my journals, some of the universal characters and themes that have come up are wise old woman, wounded healer, child, the journey or quest, villain, explorer, and hero/heroine. There have been nightmares as well as dreams filled with challenges and struggles. It is important to remember as we unpack our encounters with our inner selves that there are both personal and collective meanings for the imagery and symbolic messages that become apparent.

The ability to see and discern is deepened the more we repeat a meditative practice of observation and the letting go of our limited interpretations in order for sacred knowledge and wisdom to emerge. In this way, synchronicities become the meaningful signs or omens that indicate our "lenses" are open, or opening. Now the living archetypal energies of the Otherworld are able to send light through the fabric of the natural world and moon-shaped symbols in the sky to assist us along the way toward individuation.

Journey Exercise

The first step in recognizing synchronicities is to practice awareness either through a meditative practice or reflecting with deep curiosity. What pressing internal question has formed from your curiosity? Write your question in your journal or sketch an image that represents the query. Hold space for your question, watch for a sign, and trust that a synchronicity will emerge.

Journey Question

Write about how your answer appeared to you. Did it come through nature, working on a poem or creating artwork, or as a coincidental conversation with a stranger? Did it appear as a gut feeling, an emotion, or did the person you are thinking about contact you? Be open to these synchronistic moments. Observe and allow a connection to be made.

Chapter 7

Propping Open the Door

WE ARE IN A MOMENT OF HISTORY WHEN THE UNIQUE GIFTS OF highly sensitive persons, intuitives, and empaths are needed more than ever. Our modern society gives preferential treatment to individuals who generally are extroverted. That is to say, people who focus on the external world, often show high energy and enthusiasm, process their thinking aloud, love positive feedback, and thrive on social interaction. This partiality is because the majority of the population tend to have these or similar personality traits. It is logical, then, that society gravitates toward this character type.

Many empaths, though not all, identify with a more introverted way of relating. An orientation to the interior world gives us time to think through questions and process our answers. We are deeply curious as well as passionately persuasive when describing what we love. Empaths tend to have powerful intuitions about what is happening or about to happen. We feel especially connected to nature and absorb energy from the environment and people, which tends to make us emotional sponges. Because introverts are inclined to process internally and slowly think things through, it is not surprising that our senses are inundated, constantly processing, and overwhelmed as we quietly hold our thoughts to ourselves.

Historically, the innate ability to embody the feelings of sentient beings or to perceive the energetic vibrations of the earth were typically distrusted. Consequently, it is not unusual to trace our habit to repress these natural gifts, especially if we grew up in a family that found empathic gifts or highly sensitive skills peculiar or perhaps abnormal. Intentionally or unintentionally, we were taught to suppress our aptitudes to sense resonance in the land, to intuit the energies of people around us, to have special relationships to plants and animals, or how to uniquely illuminate dream messages. Indeed, family lineages that carry these traits and intuitive practices learned to safeguard them.

If learning to stay hidden becomes a deeply held practice of an individual or family, these strong psychic abilities seemingly fade from our consciousnesses over time. Jung would say that unused, unappreciated, and suppressed patterns retreat into the shadow of the unconscious until we are ready to stand face-to-face in their presence again. He writes, "The shadow is a living part of the personality and therefore wants to live with it in some form. It cannot be argued out of existence or rationalized into harmlessness." Empaths may occasionally notice a random aha moment or a burst of insight, and not recognize these times as glimpses of our intuitive gifts. Spending a lifetime or possibly lifetimes ignoring, suppressing, and distrusting our basic, core selves—our inner wisdom—can easily lead to a personal imbalance and inner disharmony, perhaps even illness.

In truth, these intrinsic, indelible gifts are not only real, they are the missing ingredients needed in our world to decipher the multilayered complications we all face. Being attuned with and keeping our hearts open to messages from our personal unconscious, the collective unconscious, as well as signs from the natural world offers another way of being, of living in balance.

The thirteenth-century Sufi mystic Rumi gave us advice. More than seven hundred years later, it is still not too late to heed his guidance. Rumi's poem implores, "The breezes at dawn have secrets to tell you.\Don't go back to sleep!\You must ask for what you really want.\Don't go back to sleep!\People are going back and forth across the doorsill where the two worlds touch,\The door is round and open.\Don't go back to sleep!"

It is the empath and highly sensitive person who can read the signs to which Rumi refers. We are meant to be souls at the edges, not entangled in the brambles. Our unique abilities to communicate are desperately needed in the current global ecological climate. Earth's landscape has tremendous wisdom to share with those who are able to translate that message. Intuitives can feel and sense in such a way that they are able to model for others with informed leadership. Our goose bumps, gut feelings, and instinctive impressions are an important inner guidance system essential for us to articulate. Tuning into dreams and the symbolic language of the Otherworld is a treasure beyond value. Keeping this precious talent to ourselves is not serving the greater community. "Don't go back to sleep!"

Lurking in the Shadows

Think about how long we as empaths have hidden our gifts personally and collectively. This penchant for being undercover may be something we learned or a pattern passed down to us from previous generations. The unaccepted and rejected parts of ourselves, our psyches, burrow deeply in our shadow selves and then drag behind us like unwanted baggage. Identifying, engaging, and liberating our shadows are essential to getting our powers back. There are positive aspects to the shadow, such as our empathic gifts. And there are the frustrations, angers, and fears. It is all there unconsciously impacting our lives. It takes courage to look at ourselves squarely and hug ourselves at the same time. But it is very doable and important work if we empaths are going to be the healing presences so needed right now in our world. Befriending our shadows can help us learn how to discern which are the negative energies of others that we sense as empaths and what parts are our own hurting inner selves. Facing these hidden shadow aspects hold the key to our inner balance and well-being.

Listen, observe, and allow whatever wants to unveil itself. Because on the other side of our fears is the conviction and sense of rightness that we seek. It is important to take back our powers from what is keeping us stuck and permit ourselves to move forward.

What Can You Do?

I made myself a magic wand. There is no reason why fairy tales and childhood stories should be the only bearers of this all-important symbol. I am not suggesting that we wave an enchanted baton, and it instantly gathers all the scattered parts of our psyches into the integrated whole we seek. It takes work. It is both intense and rewarding to face ourselves and bring together those parts that are hidden in plain sight.

A wand is a representational scepter symbolizing the power of the inner wisdom we already carry. We need to give ourselves the authority to hold it. Wands come in many forms, including crystals, amulets, meditative altars, sacred beads, and pendulums. I'm not afraid to feel these wisdom keeper tools in my hands as I meditate. Holding them brings me out of my head into my body. But it is not the tangible object that holds the power; it is we who embody it.

Some therapists are trained to work specifically with individuals who are empaths and highly sensitive. If there is healing required from past trauma or from consequences due to suppressing who we were born to be, this may require an in-depth process. Personal and spiritual life coaches help explore the unique genius you have to offer the community and how to express those gifts. There are spiritual companions who are trained in contemplative practices and viewing the world through a mystical lens. I believe that connecting with soul is a missing ingredient in the lives of many of us today. Certified dream coaches are particularly trained in dreamwork either for one-to-one interactions or in a group format. There are support groups designed especially for empaths and highly sensitive persons. These are some of the opportunities to listen, observe, explore, and do our inner work as empaths.

Hearing the Crow Make a Ruckus

I am emboldened by the words of poet Mary Oliver when she reflects, "Listen, are you breathing just a little and calling it a life?" The crow and other messenger birds summon us to get quiet, listen, and to tap our inner wells of wisdom. Be open and willing to receive. Curiosity and practicing awareness are important characteristics of the explorer. And don't forget to breathe.

It is a soul's homecoming awaiting us. Our inner wisdom is speaking to us through our night dreams and our day visions, intuitions, the natural world, as well as the whisperings from our ancestral legacies.

Listen for the messages awaiting you in the unexpected breeze, the sound of ocean waves, the fire of passionate flashpoints in your life, and the vibrations of the land. They will help you decipher the code of this ancient wisdom. You are needed.

There is a crack in the hidden doorway and light is shining through.

Glossary

Imbolc (pronounced *im-bolk*)—A traditional Gaelic festival celebrated sundown February 1 to February 2. It observes the beginning of spring and rebirth. It is a time for gathering energy and awakening.

Lia naofa (pronounced *leea neefa*)—A sacred stone meaningful to the holder.

Liminal—Derived from the Latin word "limen," meaning a border or doorway between one thing and another; an in-between space connecting what is known and what is hidden.

Otherworld—An understanding of the Celtic Otherworld is a place beyond the veil of our conscious awareness yet contiguous with our physical realities. It communicates with us through dreams, symbols, music, and archetypal images.

Samhain (pronounced *Sah-win*)—A traditional Gaelic festival celebrated October 31 to November 1. It represents the new year in the Celtic calendar, a season observing introspection and letting go of what is no longer needed. It is the beginning of winter, and entering the darkness.

Seanchaí (pronounced *Shan-a-hee*)—An Irish storyteller, particularly in the oral tradition. Someone who preserves old tales through the art of storytelling.

Selkie (pronounced *Sell-key*)—A Celtic mythological figure that takes the form of a seal and can also take human form.

Self—According to Jung, the self (with a lowercase s) is regarded as the ego or the center of consciousness, while the Self (capital S) is seen as the sacred unification of consciousness and the unconscious.

Thin Places—Locations on Earth where the veil between the worlds is believed to be delicate and more accessible. You could say a mystical place.

References

Blackie, S. *If Women Rose Rooted*. Tewkesbury: September Publishing, 2016.

Bourgeault, Cynthia. *Eye of the Heart, A Spiritual Journey into the Imaginal Realm*. Boulder: Shambhala Publications, Inc., 2020.

Bowers, Cathy Smith. *The Abiding Image, Inspiration and Guidance for Beginning Writers, Readers, and Teachers of Poetry*. Winston-Salem: Press 53, LLC, 2020.

Bruteau, B. *God's Ecstasy, The Creation of a Self-Creating World*. Chestnut Ridge: The Crossroad Publishing Company, 1997.

Grice, K. *The Archetypal Cosmos, Rediscovering the Gods in Myth, Science and Astrology*. Edinburgh: Floris Books, 2010.

Ingerman, S., and L. Roberts. *Speaking with Nature, Awakening to the Deep Wisdom of the Earth*. Rochester: Bear & Company, 2015.

Jung, C. G. *Synchronicity*. Princeton: Princeton University Press, 1973.

Keating, Thomas. *Intimacy with God, An Introduction to Centering Prayer*. Chestnut Ridge: The Crossroad Publishing Company, 2009.

Kindred, G. *Earth Wisdom, a Heartwarming Mixture of the Spiritual, the Practical, and the Proactive*. Carlsbad: Hay House, Inc., 2004.

MacEowen, F. *The Celtic Way of Seeing, Meditations on the Irish Spirit Wheel*. Novato: New World Library, 2007.

Merton, T. *Contemplative Prayer*. Garden City: Image Books, 1971.

O'Donohue, J. *Anam Cara, A Book of Celtic Wisdom*. New York: Harper Collins, 1998.

Ó Duinn, Seán. *Where Three Streams Meet, Celtic Spirituality*. Blackrock: Columba Press, 200o.

O'Meara, B., and K. Ward, editors. *Soul Seekers, An Irish Anthology of Celtic Shamanism*. Dublin: Acrobat Design & Publishing, 2019.

Orloff, Judith. *The Empath's Survival Guide, Life Strategies for Sensitive People*. Louisville: Sounds True, 2017.

Paintner, Christine Valters. *Eyes of the Heart, Photography as a Christian Contemplative Practice*. Notre Dame: Sorin Books, 2013.

Shainberg, C. *Kabbalah and the Power of Dreaming, Awakening the Visionary Life*. Rochester: Inner Traditions, 2005.

Suzuki, Shunryu. *Zen Mind, Beginner's Mind*. New York: Weatherhill, 1970.

Taylor, J. *The Wisdom of Your Dreams*. New York: Penguin Group, 1992.

About the Author

Katharine Donovan Kane is a certified Wayfinder Life Coach. She is equally qualified as a guide in dream exploration and spiritual companionship. Her passion as an empath is to help other highly sensitive persons to recognize their inner wisdom and share it with the world. Katharine resides in Takoma Park, Maryland. She can be reached through her website at www.kdkane.com.

Printed in the United States
by Baker & Taylor Publisher Services